# THE DOOMED BRIDEGROOM

# THE DOOMED BRIDEGROOM

— A Memoir —

## MYRNA KOSTASH

NeWest Press
Edmonton

**Canadian Cataloguing in Publication Data**
Kostash, Myrna.
 The doomed bridegroom

 ISBN 1-896300-38-3
 I. Title.
 PS8571.O882S66 1998      C818'.5407      C98-910685-3
 PR9199.3.K65D66 1998


Editor for the Press: Smaro Kamboureli
Cover and interior design: Brenda Burgess

NeWest Press gratefully acknowledges the support of the Canada Council for the Arts for our publishing program; the Department of Canadian Heritage.

The Canada Council  Le Conseil des Arts
FOR THE ARTS  DU CANADA
SINCE 1957  DEPUIS 1957

Printed and bound in Canada

NeWest Publishers Limited
Suite 201, 8540-109 Street
Edmonton, Alberta T6G 1E6

# TABLE OF CONTENTS

# PREFACE

— I —

*J*n feminist conversation in the early 1970s—"speaking bitterness"—I learned that the Sexual Revolution was a fraud; that the sexual permissiveness of the late 1960s had been a trap for women lured by the patriarchy, with slogans of liberation, into inorgasmic sex with feckless and woman-hating men in long hair and sandals.

"Goodbye to the dream," wrote Robin Morgan in a malediction of the male left in 1970, "that being in the leadership collective will get you anything but gonorrhea." I even joined the chorus, being published in literary journals with quasi-documentary exposés of love affairs gone bad and the announcement in one such piece that "the hunt for the phallus that would wound [me] perfectly was over. [I] had been a virgin all along . . . and a virgin [I] was still, hallelujah," as though sexual disappointment was much too high a price to pay for growing up.

I did not linger long in those circles and the fantasy of virginity soon functioned merely as a literary conceit. The disappointment and deception had been real enough, not to mention the inextinguishable anguish about the routine cruelty inflicted on women's bodies and souls by men around the world. But I otherwise found uncongenial the argument of women, in the aftermath of the male-dominated political conflagrations of the 1960s, that, as Morgan put it, *in the light men are all the same*.

Heterosexual couplings, these women argued well into the 1980s, were "dismal" with the erotic selfishness and inefficiency of the male lover. They extolled instead the pleasuring superiority of lesbian sex (and even of masturbation), and of the sexual utopia of a transformed sexuality in which intercourse cedes to "outercourse." Where once feminism had analyzed and theorized the material politics of sex and gender, building a case for the liberation of women from historical necessity, now the talk was all of revulsion and outrage and pain around (hetero)sex itself, as though the act of coitus, and not society or history, were the source of women's subordination.

No, I protested, this is not how I remember it. What I remember was that, because of the Pill, the counterculture of peace-and-love-making, and the international movement against the war in Vietnam, I lived a young woman's life utterly different from the vast majority of women's lives that had preceded me. I unapologetically assumed I had a right to pleasure, excitement, and the beat of my own drum—desires no longer prettified by Harlequin romances of marriage and motherhood. At the same time, thanks to the much-heralded struggles of masses of abused men and women in Asia, Africa, and Latin America against Yankee imperialism, the link had been made between their necessary heroism and our voluntary refusal of family life, consumerism, and machismo. It was a small but dramatic exodus from the post-war middle class into communes and collectives, free love and free families, revolutionary manifestos and raucous demonstrations in which we felt the exhilarating power of our massed youth and passion.

What I remember is being always, almost without a break, in love.

In *The Demon Lover*, the unreconstructed Robin Morgan in 1989 critiques the enduring propaganda of the hero myth: "There he stands," she writes of the militant IRA Provo, the Weatherman, the Red Brigadisto, the warrior of the Spear of the Nation: "young, lean, garbed in black, his face in shadow or masked by a balaclava, his gestures swift and economical as a predatory cat's, his muscled body not only bearing the magic tools of death but a magic tool of death itself, his commitment total. He is a fanatic of dedication, a mixture of impetuosity and discipline; he is desperate and therefore vulnerable; he is totally at risk and therefore brave; he is an idealist and yet a hardened realist. Most of all, he is someone wholly given over to a passion. But his passion is death. He is what passes for manhood."

What strikes me is the particular *quality* of her observation — a contempt that resonates nevertheless with echoes of her younger, hungry, desiring self, the one who admired and lusted after such men at the same time as resenting and fearing them.

These heroes are magnificently present in their bodies. They represent the ideal (for both men and women) of *action* potential in their physical readiness, a physicality mediated by their social and political commitments. Canadian labour activist Miriam Edelson writes frankly about this in "Letting Go of the Union Label: The Feminization of a Macho Myth": "Some of these men [labour union activists] pack a powerful physical attraction. They are earthy men. Men of action. I need not intellectualize this. It is a deep and visceral response to those who exert power, occasionally demonstrate self-knowledge, and display proud, peacock-like loveliness. Ah, but enough on this. I can only remind myself to leave my libido at home as I experience the longest bout of spring fever since Grade 13."

*The Demon Lover* is awesome with self-contained power and discipline, and gothically beautiful with his doom carried in his body like spore of predestination. Add to this the thrill of identification with his socialist revolutionary politics — think of the perfection of the leonine-headed Che on posters in left-wing bedrooms around the world — and our fate as women in love was sealed. "I realize," Morgan continues, a little too correctly, "that I do not want other women here. I want to save them from this." But she also *wants* to be the one chosen. "*I want to be the only one.*

Meeting after meeting I go to the bathroom and vomit. I tell myself it's the stress of revolution."

Not all of us want to evacuate these demon-lovers from our bodies nor retreat optimistically, like Morgan, into the safety of the marriage bond. The rebel hero, after all, is not for marrying. He is the transgressive par excellence. His is a free spirit, nurtured in the oppositional state, unavailable to the claims of intimacy. This is all the more enticing, exciting—the challenge of the male just out of love's reach. And romantic: Eros's animation fuelled by the sweet torments of elusive and transient couplings snatched from the agenda of the hero's higher calling. His lovers are thus spared that detumescence in the "calm of coupledom" that British feminist Elizabeth Wilson predicts, in *The Left and the Erotic*, as the conclusion of more sensible love-affairs. There is even a certain female pride in knowing this. As the hooker said to Jack Nicholson in *Carnal Knowledge*: "It takes a true woman to understand that the purest form of love is to love a man who denies himself to her. . . . He has no need for her because he has himself."

— II —

*July 1987, Vancouver*

*Reading L's journal. Pages of unfocused, high-flown feminist enthusiasm—her literate but woozy vocabulary of enlightenment—which suddenly and powerfully comes to ground in a dramatic narrative of losing her man. Her middle-aged lover has fallen in love with a student. Now L's feminist vocabulary deserts her and we are sucked into the language of rage, vengeance, malice, jealousy, scorn, fear, the Anglo-Saxon vocabulary. We are mired in and face to face with not a feminist paragon but with a woman in pain before whom the spectre of loneliness has just reared itself, and so she howls.*

*I am thinking while I am reading that this is how it feels, to be a middle-aged woman and to have had perhaps one's last lover: this is it, there will* not be others. *What is she to do—cede the game to the younger women and, in the serenity of her menopause, uninterfered with, embrace the crone within? This makes my heart ache. I'm thinking that I once had L's feelings, a decade ago, when I was still in my thirties, when I was thinner, my belly flatter, my breasts higher, my hair not yet grey. When the flesh of my face did not gather in faint pouches of cheek and chin and the tender skin under my eyes did not gather in crinkles, as they did yesterday when I bent over my compact mirror (thinking: so this is the face of a middle-aged woman, hovering over her lover in bed).*

*Now I turn lovers into friends and, years after the affairs, into inspirations for creative writing where they arouse my compassion, not need. This is the price of peace: disengagement from the womanly disturbances.*

— III —

So my "agenda" for *The Doomed Bridegroom* may very well be to explore the erotic possibilities of female heterosexual desire after the ashes have cooled on the Sexual Revolution—after my cohort has disappeared into marriage, parenthood, divorce, celibacy, death; after all the changes have been rung on sexual transgressiveness and fragmentation; while the world is hellbent for leather to the globalized post-Marxian despair of greed and digitization.

— IV —

Draft application to Maclean-Hunter Arts Journalism program, Banff, 1992: "In a series of 'auto-fictions' I am exploring the eroticism associated with suffering and martyrdom, particularly as they were lived out in the political dramas of the Cold War and New Left. As someone who came simultaneously to politics and sexuality in the 1960s, I am intrigued by the inextricability of political and sexual arousal and the ways in which I am drawn, over and over again, in sympathies of desire, to heroic figures in the extremity of resistance and sacrifice. Because of ten years' worth of travel in eastern and southern Europe, these sympathies are now represented by an obsession to narrate a personal history of arousal by transgressive men, alive and dead, in Poland, Ukraine and Greece."

— v —

The arousal is specific, located in dramas of courage, despair, and failure in countries wracked by a certain complex of cultural and political history. The Jewish boy in a political science class in Edmonton and then in a California prison is the avatar but after him come the men of the "other Europe" (they are always there, in that otherness, and not in Paris, say, or Dublin), usually speaking a Slavic language or one outside the Latin alphabet, trapped in long histories played out at the overlapping territories of East and West, formed by brutal events, and re-formed by their own nervy dream of what is possible if only one "lives in the truth."

In travelling among them I discovered that there were historical reference points that were at least as powerful triggers of my arousal as were the flashpoints of the western New Left: Bolshevik revolutionary songs, the Cyrillic alphabet scratched in clandestine poems, ruined Orthodox monasteries, doomed peasant insurgents, heroic labourers in the mines and mills of Soviet bosses, not to mention the deep attractiveness of young people of my own time, plotting hi-jinks and confrontations in the brazen theatre of the autonomous imagination. All of these were caught up, for me, in huge swirls of historical narrative that threw Slavs down to the Adriatic, Tatars across the Black Sea, Cossacks into

the steppes, Byzantine monks to Rus, Ottomans to Belgrade —
and Reds everywhere.

Martin, for instance, is in Prague under Soviet "occupation," a
complete man in a parallel world of perfect non-compliance with
power, signatory to a dangerous document, waiting his turn to
go to prison. Igor was in Kiev (Kyiv), arrived from the Ukrainian
provinces, a sheaf of poems in his hand, in the very days and
months and years of the frozen 1970s when poets and historians
and choir masters disappeared from the rooms he haunted into
the silent agony of the camps. Tomaz is in Yugoslavia in the last
gasps of "workers' self-management," travelling to illegal meetings in People's Poland and People's Hungary, rousing students
at home with blueprints of a self-created future of punk, narco-
mania, and workers' strikes. These are the specifics that drew me
to them, but History held me there in an embrace of excited
camaraderie.

"But how about desire? . . . which equally can turn the nape of
your neck or the back of your hand into a sexual explosion."
Eileen Phillips, *The Left and the Erotic*

. . . I surface from sleep, but I want to go back there into my
dreams and continue the kisses. I wake up and think of raising
my face for a kiss from Martin, in the kitchen on Jecna Street.
Everyone is watching as our two bodies lean in together, press,
hold. That beautiful face, the blue eyes, the black curls. Leaning
in to be kissed, lips feasting on each other, the flesh turning
around in our mouths, fingers dancing on neck and shoulders,
hands scooping breasts. Oh Martin of Jecna Street, take me,
take me to Tabor, let us hurtle down the Moravian highway,
tell me stories of Jan Hus and his uprisings, of the bands of men
and women in possession of this countryside before they were
defeated and perished, take me in cornfields, limbs flailing near
the dead, take me in cobblestoned squares near the funeral pyres,
feed me wild berries, quench my thirst with wine.

It drives me restless and unsatisfied, this memory of Martin and me in the Jecna kitchen, laughing together, falling into each other's speech, lips brushing, and then I dash away, tearing myself away from the ghost-self who has gripped Martin in her arms.

What is this sensation in London with Igor, whose hand at my elbow to guide me through hallways at the BBC sends a thrilling *frisson* through my arms as though he had touched my nipple? And this laughing flirtatiousness of conversation? We make each other laugh; it's good. I tell him of the bar I would like to own on the Mediterranean, he could come, he would come, he'd slip in one night from far away, would sit in a corner and wait for the others to be gone, then stroll up to the wine-slopped bar, in a brown leather jacket, his hands in pockets, his face creased with fatigue. I would put out the lights and lock the doors against the soughing sea and at the top of the staircase on the way to my rooms he would take me, lay me on the floor in the starlight and take me.

In London when I step out of the van in Kensington Gardens and turn towards him and his family to say goodbye, he grabs my hand and puts his mouth to my knuckles. I realize even as I am withdrawing my hand that he wants to hold it and kiss it and, too late, I want to give it back to him, to open up its palm to his mouth, feel his tongue scratching between the fingers, to close my fingers around his chin and raise his dear funny Russian face to mine for a kiss.

*Ljubljana, May 21, 1988.* . . . Once more on the merry-go-round. The young man, perfect in his autonomy, anorectic with revolutionary discipline, whose shirt lies open on his shoulder, exposing a place where I would like to leave a kiss. Did Tomaz feel that kiss upon his shoulder, the taut, cool flesh? . . . I sit across from him at his kitchen table, the rain pouring down outside the closed shutters, and think of putting my fingers into his curly hair. I take his glasses off his bony face and look at him—this sudden blue-eyed, boyish, short-sighted gaze staring back at me. Does he want what I want? To take the candle to his narrow bed and embrace him in a narrow space while the rain rages on. . . . I wanted to say to him, "in another life I would like to be your lover," but though I never said it, even so it was insincere. That other life doesn't exist. I want *this* life, with him in *this* bed. I am intent upon seduction.

Later he writes me from various places in exile.

And now nothing. He has simply vanished from all accounting. Good. Equilibrium has been reinstated and I can begin.

# ACKNOWLEDGEMENTS

I am grateful to the Alberta Foundation for the Arts for a writer's grant which supported me in the lengthy and interrupted writing of this book. I also benefitted from a two-month Ashley Fellowship at Trent University, participation in the Maclean-Hunter Arts Journalism Seminar at the Banff Centre for the Arts and two serene weeks at the Writers' Colony organized by the Saskatchewan Writers' Guild at St. Peter's Abbey near Muenster.

I had the inestimable fortune to work with Smaro Kamboureli, enthusiastic and pitiless editor, and with the always patient, supportive, and quick-thinking staff of NeWest Press, Liz Grieve, Kathy Chiles, and Jennifer Bellward.

Chapters of this book, as they went through numerous drafts, were passed around several agreeable and attentive readers. I would like to acknowledge their contribution to the critical rethinking of my text: Nancy Burke, Chrystia Chomiak, Kathleen Flaherty, John-Paul Himka, Angela Hryniuk, Janice Kulyk Keefer, Julie Landsman, Barbara Pulling, Myroslav Shkandrij, Lida Somchynsky, and Eve Zaremba. And to Ania Andrusieczko and Bohdan Nebesio, thanks for long conversations about growing up in Poland.

Particular thanks go to Alberto Manguel and Barbara Moon for seeing, before I did, what I was doing, and for helping me get there. I am in their debt.

# MISSISSIPPI DREAMING

## — I. 1965 —

Snowbanks are heaved up along the sidewalk as I walk to campus, my boots crunching on the snowy crust of the cement. The world is very still and clear, suspended in the freezing blue air. Sucking the air down into my lungs I am thinking that I wish to be in Mississippi. I wish to be in that hot, moist place, tramping along the delta, my arms linked through black arms, on a freedom march. I do not think about how I would get there or whether anyone would have me. I do not think about the lay of the land or the expression on the faces of the white folks as I sashay through their towns nor even of the faces of the Negro men and women for whom I, Ukrainian-Canadian daughter of schoolteachers, student of Russian and French literature in a university on latitude fifty-three, make this sacrifice of my upward social mobility. I think only of how I would *feel*.

That Mississippi Delta woman is not this one crunching her way to school through the shocking whiteness of the Edmonton winter. I am not present at the scene of my own white girl's humiliation in the middle class. I am elsewhere, in the drama of strangers in pain.

In little rented bungalows near the university, in disdainful regard of the neighbouring beer-sodden "Greeks" in their fraternity houses, the members of the New Democrat Youth have parties. The frat-rats are short-haired boys in blue blazers and grey flannels who study Commerce and pre-Law. It is not that I despise them but that they do not arouse me. They are just there, in my peripheral vision, while the boys at the parties of the NDY snap and sizzle, heating up the space around them—the kitchen counter, the corner between the fridge and the wall, the steps of the front porch—with the ardour of their ideas. It is the defloration of my virginal vocabulary: oppression, class enemy, being and nothingness. Their hair falls in their eyes. Stubble roughens their cheeks. They wear sunglasses indoors and bare feet in sandals. Later they will have hair down to their shoulders and they will wrap their brown, hairless torsos in crushed velvet shirts, but now they are still in corduroy jackets and their words excite me, lift me up out of my skin, just as if their hands were on my breasts and their teeth on my tongue.

"Lenny" sits in the desk right in front of me in "Political Institutions of the Soviet Union" class. He has a fine head of thick, wavy black hair, some of it growing in stray tendrils down his neck. When he moves his head sideways, I see the nose bent gently at the bridge and the heavy lashes over his green eye. He wears a tan-coloured corduroy jacket and black jeans. He has an accent: "Gotta kwawtah foh a cuppa kawfee?" He's from the Bronx. He's a draft dodger. I sit staring at the back of his head, pulsing with admiration.

Sometimes I catch him falling asleep. On the way out of class, he begins suddenly to talk to me, as though I had started something, staring at the back of his head. He tells me he is *eating* methadrine to keep himself awake all night, writing not only his term papers but also articles for the student paper about Vietnam and the draft resistance in the United States, speeches for a rally in front of the legislature, not to mention letters to all his strung-out friends back in New York, each one of whom, it seems, is in deep shit. I imagine race riots, self-inflicted mutilations on the steps of army recruitment centres, and heroin needles in the garbage behind jazz clubs in Greenwich Village. I look around the campus coffee shop, my friends eating cinnamon buns and plugging nickels into the jukebox.

Somehow he and I will get from Poli Sci 460 to a slow walk towards the bank of the North Saskatchewan in the experimental warmth of the April sunshine, the toes of our boots getting soaked in the melting run-off, the muddy earth under the sere grass making squidging sounds under our heels.

He brags about how clever he was in coming up here to university so far north in an outpost no American authority has heard of. He feels snug here, he tells me, cosy and taken care of. He puts his arm around me as if to say he means me too, that I am part of his shelter.

There is a war in southeast Asia. I hate this war. But it has brought this boy to me and the one million Vietnamese and 58,000 American dead are yet to come. We sit cross-legged on the gymnasium floor at the teach-in, spreading maps and documents over the lines of a basketball court. Our little fingers rub together as we trace the thick black line of the Ho Chi Minh Trail. He rocks on his buttocks as we raise our fists and scream, *Hey, hey, LBJ, how many kids did you kill today?* and I can see, because his thighs are splayed open and I am interested, the bulky bulge of his crotch whose contents remain for the moment mysterious.

Eventually we will go to my bed. He is my first lover. He has small hands and feet, not much bigger than mine, but I love to squeeze his fingers when they curl up in the palm of my hand and lick their tips as they wander over my face. I take care to cultivate my feelings. When he tells me how his parents are sick about his kid brother Bennie who is living with an older woman, a Puerto Rican with two kids, I make note of his laughter and the embryonic twitch of jealousy behind my breastbone. "What a kid!" he says, "Up their asses!" as I squeeze his knee high up between my thighs, wanting to distract him.

His friends are Marxist professors and neurotic women. He

argues passionately with the men, noisy hullabaloos about vanguardism, while I sit in a corner, abashed that I have not done the reading, and leaf through old copies of *Red Flag* as though I could catch up. The women I find lying on his couch, tearing their hair and popping pills while my lover hears their confessions, kneeling beside the couch, his knees in a rubble of ashtrays, album sleeves and broken-spined paperbacks. I plead with him to send these women away, their hysterics are taking up our precious time, but he glowers at me accusingly. I am being selfish. Later he makes airplanes of their love letters and sends them flying around our bed. I think this means that I have "won."

I fly off for the summer, not realizing that I will not come back for ten years. He writes frequently, keeping me within reach of his thought processes. No one has ever talked to me like this, not even he, when he had the chance.

He reassures me that I cannot reasonably expect to learn all there is to know about making a man happy in bed in two easy lessons. There are little things any prostitute could show me but the main thing is to be honest with my emotions. I suppose his own honesty was by way of setting an example: he disclosed, "oh by the way," that he and my old room-mate had discussed the possibility of sleeping together but had concluded that would ruin a good friendship.

In a tone I find unseemingly nonchalant, he counsels me to expand my sexual repertoire — and complement our love affair — by sleeping with someone who will not be too demanding of my time and feelings, a married professor, for instance. And oh, by the way, "Lola" is in town and he'll probably make love to her but in the meantime she is popping all kinds of pills, her neuroses pour out of her, she is brainpower personified, a loner, an existentialist. I, by contrast, spoiled our sexual adventures by being altogether too passive, too virginal, lying there *being made love to* rather than being a participant in a sharing process. This was a blow to his self-esteem, but Lola, happily, is restoring it. He had hoped that in our brief four months together I would have got to really know him but, alas, it seems I was only looking at myself. Ah, ah, he is pushing all my buttons . . . I am his dear heart, he writes, his lovely soul, his love, he adores me, he kisses me, and I forgive all, knowing he is staying up all night working on a paper on the changes in the Soviet economy, auditing a computer science course, organizing a blood drive for the Vietnamese and dreaming about a "slum project" for the summer.

## — II. 1966–1970 —

I finally explode in a letter to my sister: "What sickens me is that the way he discusses the women and his affairs with them is so completely contrary to all the preaching he did for my benefit. He used to tell me that bodies and sex are meaningless and boring if the whole personality wasn't considered. Blah blah blah. I think I hate men." I say nothing of the sort to him, however, but crumble with lonesome gratitude when he writes that, without me, he feels lost, alone, immobile, there in the land of meaningless sex.

Here and there in the letters erupts the scalding confession of his guilt from his long-ago affair with his best friend's older sister. It was the first great love of his life, though, characteristically, he did not realize this until it was over and she was gone into marriage. I myself wonder, fleetingly without being able to pursue it, how much of his excoriation of my sexuality is actually about his. *Look, love, you are love,* but of course he knows he is not the man with the kind of thoughts and being I should have.

Long after I've moved on he will write that he hopes we will meet frequently and are happy together for the short time our lives are one. His last letter is written three years and two months after we became lovers. He remembers how I seemed to him the day I left town—more beautiful than he had ever seen me, head thrown back, "hair in the wind." He wants to know when I'm coming home.

— III. 1977 —

An American flag, about twenty feet by thirty feet, hung on a wall of the Customs Immigration Hall. The sight of it triggered an automatic response: the "home movies" in my head, rewinding and projecting on the back of my skull the demonstrations and sit-ins over whose dissidence the Stars and Stripes, the abominable flag, once fluttered. It could still make my palms sweat.

I filled out the Entry card and handed it over to the official. He scrutinized it. "Going to Berkeley?" An interrogation, as though I'd lied and was planning instead to go to, say, San Jose. He opened my briefcase and palpated the cosmetics bag. If one is going to Berkeley, one is up to something?

A taxi ride took me down to the lingering heart of it: Telegraph Avenue. There where the avenue conjoins with the campus, entrepreneurs had established a row of kiosks where you could buy felafels and cappuccino and take them into the sunshine of the quad. Here once, and massively, a student movement had been born also for the right to sell, in that case anti-apartheid literature. But in 1977 the students were not dusty and crumpled from sleeping overnight on the floors of deans' offices; they walked easy. Their heads swivelled, lolled on their shoulders. I thought of them, in cut-offs and running shoes, as children of the Imperium which, after the little wobble of the war in Vietnam, had returned to its normal, unanxious practices of world domination. This was why the aging draft dodgers were returning, resisters of a forgiven war, dribbling back from chilly northern provinces to California to reinherit citizenship.

California normalizes its own excesses. The bland, window-less cement walls of the Bank of America on Telegraph were said to be built in Riot Renaissance style, an allusion to the fact that some years ago rioters had systematically and repeatedly taken out the windows with bricks and bats. The rioters were gone now. The bank, windowless still, was just another bank.

On a somnolent Sunday afternoon I took the bus across the Bay, across the city, to Haight-Ashbury. I suppressed the ghost army of hippies of 1967 so that I would see what was now here — a neighbourhood in the process of being reclaimed by the indigenous, by those who had laboured to make it home. An old bum scooped out a rind of cantelope. Black youths, their transistor radio at their feet, danced like cats in a catnip bed. Someone ass-end in the air tinkered in the bowels of his Chevy. A venerable Chinese woman shuffled in canvas shoes into a grocery displaying the wilting stocks of curly-leafed greens.

I couldn't say I was exactly disappointed. Between the defaced facades of boarded-up stores, the occasional "head shop" was carrying on its necessary trade and in a coffee house yogurt shakes were being served up while a young man with long blond hair sat at a piano and sang Bob Dylan songs with a romantic intensity missing in the original version.

I took a photograph of a rather monumental wall mural. A group of black slaves, Indians, and farmers stand resolutely with the tools of their respective labour that become the gears and wheels of the proletarian shop floor that become the long black rifle in the hand of a robust woman in a red dress. At this same corner I had once crouched on my hands and knees to draw exuberant chalk festoons of psychedelic flowers. The mural on the wall was certainly not psychedelic — not signing itself insolently, solely, as a stoned high. And it seemed to me that the brown arms raised in clenched fists were a salute punch-ed out this time in history. My own fist hung uncurled on my thigh.

I arrived at Terminal Island Federal Correctional Institution in time for the head count of prisoners. All the doors had slammed and locked together. I had an hour to wait.

All the patient women, black, brown, white, were implanted in vinyl chairs, thighs spread uncomposedly, their mournful faces turned to the windows and, beyond, the chainlink fence and the sea. Children careered squealing around the rubbish containers. I read the signs warning me against aiding a prisoner to escape or bringing him narcotics and alcohol. This only provoked some baroque fantasies of derring-do at the perimeter of the chainlink fence. I walked back and forth the length of the waiting room, my heart in my throat.

The key turned in the lock and, one at a time, the men came through. The key turned, the door opened, a man stepped through, the door shut, the key turned. There was an hour of this. I stood at the edge of family reunions, staring at the door. How much could a man have changed in eight years? It was as though Lenny might have slipped through without my noticing that that was he, that man there in the baseball cap and belly overhanging the snake's head belt buckle.

But when Lenny finally stepped through he was as I remembered him. Of course, deeper lines in the face framing his upper lip, and grey hair at the temple, but it was Lenny of the long-lashed green eye, the beak nose, the barrel chest, and the dainty feet. He was wearing a white T-shirt and green army jacket and stood grinning at me from just this side the steel door.

They say a woman's first lover is the only lover; all who come after are surrogates. I had had my share of them, chasing one proud dark man after another from Toronto to London to Ibiza and back to Toronto. Thinking I was done with Lenny, I had folded him away into the box of old letters in my basement, accepting that I had grown up and fled the girl who had sat on his living room floor, weeping, as a bottle of cheap sherry, upset, dripped its sticky contents onto a pile of anti-war pamphlets. Now I remembered her, and how she had lain body and soul with this first bridegroom and pledged a kind of fidelity she had never revoked.

We put our arms around each other and walked out into the yard. Another prisoner with a little business on the side took our picture with a Polaroid camera as we sat, for all the world like holiday-makers, at a round table under a big striped umbrella, arms still around each other's shoulders. We turned away from each other's excited faces to look at the camera with opening, laughing mouths. When I look at the picture now I see clearly at our backs the chainlink fence.

I was listening to his story. He was talking of class consciousness and of the return to his social origins. He was talking of a factory and a union and a strike; he said a lot about guns and how he had lived in households of weapons and instructed Black women in self-defence and had stolen (crept through basement windows) the guns of the middle class. He was steeped in Mao: Rely on the people. When the FBI came to his house without a search warrant, he showed them the nose of a sawed-off 12 gauge shotgun, for which act he was ultimately acquitted by a jury. Rely on the people.

Then came the sequence of events that led him to prison: a fugitive in the basement, a double agent, or perhaps only someone afraid, who lacked Maoist fortitude. He had overcome his loathing, he said, of middle class revolutionaries. However, only his union buddies came to see him now. I listened carefully, for I wanted to know all about it, but what had this to do with me? Even while he made his trek back to the USA, even as he conspired with his comrades, even as he delivered speeches that the FBI duly noted, had the image of my face still floated behind his green eye?

We strolled arm in arm around the yard, watched by an armed guard up in the watchtower. On a piece of grass behind a bush I spread out the lunch I had brought, hoping to be memorable: brie, grapes, strawberry cakes, papaya juice. I wanted to live there with him on this island at the end of the road, climb within the sheets of his prisoner's bed, peel an avocado and feed him.

He told me that he was no longer proud that he had managed to slip away from the war and go up to Canada. While his class brothers died, he had pretended he too had "acted." Now he was ashamed. I pondered this. Thought of the grunts in Vietnam whose buddies had burned beside them while their own jammed M-16s poked uselessly in the air at the jungle perimeter. . . . Had Lenny come back into the belly of the beast to find some way to *be* with them, to stand beside them as they dropped? He had come to Canada, to my city, and changed my life. But now he was ashamed. My brother, my soul.

I flew away shell-shocked. I had come for a visit, but left willing to wait outside the gates, in a rented car, until he was free. I would marry him, I swore, be his bride again, the virgin at the threshold of her carnal knowledge, and be taken again and again and again, repeating ritually the first act of my body's sacrifice to the doomed bridegroom.

— IV. 1977–1978 —

At first he wrote with tenderness, warm letters full of the pleasure of our reconnection, *my dear sweet friend*, the chill routine of prison broken by the correspondence, the wan colour of his cell enlivened by the art postcards I sent him. I sent too a photograph of the little farm I'd bought, its sky a conflagration of purple and scarlet clouds piled up in the northwest. He remembered those days he lived under that sky with us, his friends, with me, his lady, his saint, his cellblock *guardian, protectress and avenger*. My portrait was there too, all mouth and eyes, *my dear sweet friend and sister*. There was no way he could possibly convey to me the reality of the cesspool in which he lived. Its grotesqueness and absurdity.

I didn't care.

Then came letters full of admonishment. He cautioned me that we were abstractions from each other's life, figments of each other's imagination. I was to beware the kindliness of my own nature: the prisoner, lean, dark-skinned, brooding, his sexuality disciplined and contained, wrings my heart with pity, arouses me. This was not real. What was real was the killing in the yard two weeks ago and the stabbing last week, tension, aggravation, friends locked down. The three thousand pages of his files from the FBI. Cold coffee in styrofoam, cold tortillas from the canteen, a wet towel hanging from a nail.

I knew he was right but I didn't care. I persisted. There was the breeze that came off the ocean and blew our exploratory sentences into bits, his comely ears, the blunt shape of his shoulders under his thin T-shirt, his lip wettened by his tongue, the arch of my back as I tried to get closer to him in the hug he gave me good-bye.

I was the woman in love. I had a consort. He may yet have turned away from me but I had chosen him. It was just a question now of history dragging us together. I could wait.

So I would come to his bed like this, he lying heavily, arms across his chest. I would peel back the blanket, and he would reach up to put out the light and hide me there, curled up between his thighs, and very very quietly, without a squeak, he would swing himself gently into me and rock himself to sleep. My brother, my soul.

He used to say—I have the letters somewhere—that there had always got to be a way for us to be together. There it was.

— V. 1978 —

He wrote on a peaceful, lazy Sunday afternoon, a year later, after his release that, on such a day, dreaming helps him get beyond his aloneness. It is my birthday and he is thinking of me, of my new peace and contentment with myself and my work—but he's just rambling, so he'll just wish me happiness, on my birthday and forever.

As for his own situation, in his spare couple of minutes a week, he's trying to sell real estate to pay for the forty acres he just bought. But even crazier is what's going on in his union—the guy shot and killed at a union meeting, racist union officers complaining about "Latinos, trying to take over the union." He's still looking for steady work.

Yeah, he's still trying to understand "everything," how class relations can be changed and which classes "benefit from what" but, hey, that doesn't mean we can't all go play among the flowers, make love in a meadow, get stoned, and head off into the sunset on our motorcycles.

Six months later he married his lawyer.

— VI. 1987 —

I in my green Beetle driving up to the cabin, driving ruts through the tall weeds in the yard, the sun launched half way up the sky. Bees buzz lazily in the purple borage, droning in the red poppies, gently fucking the blue clover. It's cool inside the cabin. I throw open the windows to let in the heat; the sheets on the bed are cool, I throw off the covers to let in the heat. I lie down to roll in the cool and then in the heat.

There's a curling postcard, splattered in fly shit, above the bed. Another lover had sent it, with (unattributed) poem. I've been reading it since 1969 and still can't figure it out. But it plays me like music.

> But ah, alas, alas, Lottipo
> the mushy marshes, those tree-lined woods
> the so-small journeying and the travellers

*these too and all else, alas, are only real.*
*So may we remember once again*
*how the grasses cause the wind to move.*
*And that we love! is this not proof of something?*

I look out the east-facing window towards the swell of land that rolls to the North Saskatchewan. I have hung up my straw hat by the rickety door. A mother squirrel races back and forth across the ceiling rafters, raucous and affronted by my presence. She will do this for a couple of days and then I will win.

The yellow buffalo bean is everywhere and that strange red plant, Old Man's Whiskers, and purple vetch, which mother says makes cow's milk sweet. You see the things I know?

Last night it rained, tap-tapping a lullaby above me on the roof. Now sluggish flies die on the tabletop, on their back, kicking all their legs.

One cluttered room for home. Bits of candle, postcards from travelling friends, the county map, the dried yellow roses from my sister's wedding. On the window sill the license plate from the motorcycle I say that some lover and I rode from Mendocino on our way to the corrida, and to the end of the bull, the heat, and us.

— VII.—

When the affair was finishing, we would find ourselves dancing in the frenzy not of crazy love but of a drug. I was wearing a green blouse and black miniskirt. He still wore his corduroy jacket. It was a Christmas party. I would not be going to Mississippi. I would never go to Mississippi.

# THE COLLABORATORS

*N*afplion, on the Peloponnese, in late May of 1981. The woman, a Canadian in her mid-thirties, was vacationing in Greece, which she had last visited in 1969. In 1969 she had visited Sounion to see the sun set behind the pillars of the temple of Poseidon and was now ashamed to realize that, at that time, beyond the splendid view, lay a little treeless and waterless prison island where Greeks were sweating, weeping, and dying under the curse of the Junta.

There was no correcting this sort of oversight, she thought.

She was a solitary traveller. In quiet Nafplion, people seemed content to go about their business and leave her to hers. From her modest hotel room window she had a view of red-tiled roofs and domes and, beyond them, the blue mountains of the Argolid. In the late afternoon she would sit on the hotel terrace and look at these mountains. She would be amazed that there, just beyond the first ridge, amid the wreckage of the acropolis of Mycenae, stood the royal hall of the house of Agamemnon and, somewhere in the rubble, the bath in which Clytemnestra had murdered her consort at the end of his journey, across the stony plain from Argos, home from the war at Troy. She was thinking that, depending on whose side you took — Clytemnestra's or Agamemnon's — you could reveal a lot about how you see history, its several versions.

She could be seen having a yoghurt at a battered table in a milk shop or lying on the beach or strolling through the narrow streets glimpsing, between garden gates left ajar, tiny courtyards of lemon trees and bougainvillaea and geraniums. No one took much notice.

One day someone did. It was a warm evening and she had gone early to a seaside taverna so she could have the place more or less to herself. She sat slumped in the canvas chair, sipping wine and looking out to the water. After a few minutes, a man sat down at the table next to hers, seating himself so he was looking in her direction.

— * —

*Did that make you uncomfortable?*
Yes. I knew he was looking at me. Suddenly I was no longer a woman alone but a woman without a man.
*Did you leave?*
I asked the waiter for a pen. I wanted to look busy, occupied. I took out a little notebook in which I was keeping track of my expenses and I began converting all the drachmas into dollars. But then the waiter came back for his pen. Immediately the man at the next table jumped up and offered his. In English.
*Did you take it?*
I decided I would. The man who was offering it was neither particularly young nor good-looking. For several minutes he left me alone. I was just getting relaxed again when he blurted out, "Are you a writer?" It seemed an honest question.
*At least more interesting than "Where are you from?"*
And then: "What do you write about?" I waved my hands around and spoke carefully, but I didn't think all of it was registering. Would he even know these words: prairie, Ukrainian, Cree, counterculture, New Left, sisterhood?

— * —

This Greek place was nothing like her homeplace. Here were people so deeply rooted in their communal past that they shared a physiognomy, carried the same body. Here there were emigrants, not immigrants, and there were no hippies (except those on the road, overland from London and Paris to Kabul and cheap hashish) and no free-for-alls in campus offices, nor any exultant parade of Sapphic young women. Here were, instead, students trapped in the searchlights beamed from the army tanks that rolled over the iron gates of the Polytechnic and into the forecourt, the machine guns following the beams of light. Dead students, and women who brought dowries into their marriage and handed them over to the husband in the kafenion who was playing cards and losing. So she tried that other vocabulary, the common currency of earlier generations, and said she wrote about oppression, exploitation, resistance, and struggle. She winced, thinking she sounded imbecilic.

*Did he wince too?*
On the contrary. By now he was sitting at my table, astride a backwards chair, and he laid his hand enthusiastically on my arm practically shouting, "I know what you mean! At the university I was a Communist too. I *am* a Communist."
*Wasn't that kind of dangerous to say to a perfect stranger?*
He didn't seem to give a damn. He seemed excited by this kind of talk. Then he whisked me away to a club where we sat on hard, narrow benches, and ordered a bottle of wine. We toasted each other and our absent friends and our youth and the shades of Che Guevara and Ho Chi Minh and Jimi Hendrix. A man at the front was singing songs of Mikis Theodorakis (another Communist), in fact the whole club was singing. My Communist too, his eyes shut, a hand on each knee.

*Love that Party!*
These songs, he told me, were about partisans and squatters and dead students, about the death of Garcia Lorca, about the execution of Communists and the roses that grew up in the craters left behind by the bullets in the wall. I told him that I had never heard such songs before. I mean, who would sing them?

— * —

In the morning he fetched her in his white Fiat and they drove to the nearest beach, quite deserted. It was a very clear morning, almost still the only sound that of the pebbles at the shoreline rolling leisurely in the retreat of the little lapping waves. She had her bathing suit on under her clothes. She undressed and walked slowly into the sea. She slid into it and swam back and forth in a line parallel with the shore, conscious, from the moment she had unbuttoned her shirt, of the regard of the man who, leaning on his arm, was watching her. This was not entirely unsettling. Later, curled up into the bend of his body, the sun heating her flesh, she felt she was desirable. He stroked her hair and called her his comrade.

They had lunch at a taverna at the other end of the beach. She was learning to like this sort of meal: cool, resinated wine out of the barrel, a slab of white cheese, chopped tomatoes in olive oil and oregano, a plate of small fried fish which she dismembered with her fingers when he laughed at her knife and fork. Then they drove away to his hotel—she could come with him or not—and, the shutters pulled down against the mid-afternoon sun, they made love. He fell asleep but she was not used to afternoon naps. She wished she had a book. His back was turned to her. She didn't want to wake him up by leaning over to look into his face.

The second night they were together, they had supper in a fish taverna where he immediately became embroiled in what seemed like a furious argument with several old fishermen at the next tables. From the look on their faces and the emphasis in his voice, she took them to be politically hostile. She had heard about an old fisherman in Nafplion who from time to time would find his nets cut. He was a Communist.

— * —

*So who was your lover?*
Kostas Karapanayiotis. It took me awhile to memorize.
*What was he doing in Nafplion?*
He was an organizer for the socialist party, PASOK. He explained it was his job to travel to the villages in the Peloponnese and drum up support for the Fall elections. Everyone was expecting the left to make a strong showing. Even Communists were going to vote for PASOK, just to get the right out of government.
*Did Kostas have political ambitions of his own?*
I don't think so. He struck me simply as someone terribly committed to doing what he could to spread the gospel, so to speak, and very much aroused by political debate. He thought the socialists had a very good chance of winning, but he also expected the Americans would move immediately to destabilize a left-wing government.
*Not entirely implausible.*
Listen, he was so convinced of this scenario that he had also joined an underground group of Communists in Patras, militants who met regularly in secret to train for guerrilla warfare. The memory of seven years of the Junta was still fresh. I understood this.

— * —

On the night of the third day together, he told her he might have to leave very early the next morning for Patras. An urgent meeting of the cell. While she was still half-asleep he slipped out to make a call from the phone booth in the street below their hotel room. And then drove away. She didn't see him for a week.

She mooned about in the hot streets of Nafplion and lingered at the seaside taverna, remembering how they had torn the little fried fish and stuffed the fingerfuls of flesh into each other's mouth, taken long swills of retsina, leaving grease on the rim of the glasses. How he had laughed and laid his head on her shoulder but was all seriousness when they talked, slowing down to find the words. She tried to fit them into what she knew of the history of this often wretched country—a people abandoned to semi-literacy and cowed by generations of tyrants in the schools, the courts, the police stations, not to mention at home, in the family. A population that made its way under the eye of the CIA and that broke off, at least once every generation, into fragments of furious political violence that was futile in its consequences. She thought of blood-soaked village squares, ghost armies, and unmarked graves.

The songs filled in their conversational gaps. He had a big black case in his car and he pulled one ragged cassette out after another and played her Greek songs. There was one about a partisan of that Resistance still without memorial in Greece, lined up against a wall, about to be shot by the fascists. Tearing away the blindfold from his eyes, the partisan sings out that he wants to *see* the light of freedom to come in the moment of his death. Kostas wound and rewound the tape, played the dying partisan again and again and again until she was almost, unbearably, aroused.

He had a Bob Dylan tape too but for the first time in fifteen years she did not believe that, at that moment, the words to "Desolation Row" were adequate to anything.

She was now frantically in love with him and would have been happy to spend the next ten years hurtling along these highways, running the same circle of towns, villages and beaches, hotel rooms and tavernas, around and around the Peloponnese while Kostas fulfilled his obligations to the Greek revolution that lay just ahead. In the next town, or the one after that.

The next time she saw him he invited her to join him on a trip to some western Peloponnesian villages. They drove through Corinth and Patras (she wondered if they might stop surreptitiously at the cell HQ) and turned south towards Olympia, his one hand on the steering wheel, the other alternately pulling out big hand-fuls of cherries from the bag that lay between them and resting lightly on her thigh (her skirt pulled up to catch the breeze from the window).

In Olympia he paid in advance for their room, made love to her and then took her to a café where he ordered ouzo and left her, explaining he had to go back to Patras. By now Patras had become focused in her mind as a small house on the outskirts of town where, very late at night, six, ten, fifteen men of all ages, with moustaches and smoking suicidely, shouting and waving their arms in the chop-chop Greek manner, plotted their strate-gies for the defence of the Greek republic. She imagined, there in the darkened anteroom, heavy wooden boxes holding AK-47s from Bulgaria.

He was back in Olympia the next morning and they continued their journey south. In the early evening, near Pylos, he turned off onto a secondary road that went straight up into the moun-tains. They stopped at the first village where he explained he had a meeting arranged with some farmers. For three hours she sat on a wobbly aluminum chair, sipping ouzo and munching a large quantity of peanuts, while at the other side of the square a small group of men, the gnarled and the smooth, in and out of caps, feet planted in dusty boots, listened and argued as Kostas held forth in the diminishing light. From time to time he would pull papers from his briefcase and pass them around but the expres-sion on their faces scarcely wavered as they perused them. The only woman she saw was a middle-aged crone in black, side-saddle on a donkey ambling across the far side of the square. She wondered idly how this woman was going to vote.

It got dark and she began to fret. This was their last night. Tomorrow she would fly to Athens and to Toronto, and leave him to his mysterious errands in the night-time, his rehearsals for an uprising, a noisy intervention into the silence.

But this was also important, she admitted, this agitation in the village square. At home she knew no men who did such a thing. Whom would they agitate?

— * —

*Was he married?*
He had a fiancée, Fotini. He wore her ring.
*When was he going to marry her?*
After the election, if at all. He hated the idea of marrying in church. The socialists had promised to introduce civil marriage.
*A man of some principles.*
He had serious reservations about marrying, period. Or having children. Considering his commitment to revolutionary politics, more or less clandestine.
*Did you feel guilty towards Fotini?*
Not at all. I didn't want to marry him. She did. But he spoke of her as a nice and simple girl who wanted the marriage to make her parents happy. Sometimes he spoke of their engagement as a kind of propitiation for having slept with her.
*It sounds rather self-serving.*
Let's put it this way. He told me he couldn't find, among Greek women, a companion with whom to share his political values. I sympathized with his frustration.
*Companion? Is that what you were?*
I was his lover.

— ✳ —

They sat in the heat of the mid-afternoon on fragments of tumbled marble columns at Olympia. The earth was grassy and spongy with pine needles and shaded by ancient pines. There were crickets. And Kostas's soft voice recreating the antique games, the oily bodies straining for the prize. All of them, for these Olympic days at least, *Greeks*. "I am not a nationalist," he said, "but I am a Greek."

Then he was gone again to Patras and left her to sleep forlornly alone. She thought of him on his treks through the mountains. To give him company, she pictured a shepherd and his goats and heard the bleating and his rough calls echo up and down the sered, narrow valleys. She saw an old woman leading her donkey bearing a bundle of twigs wrested from the mountain scrub. She saw a priest and bridal party climbing to the shrine of the Panagia while down other paths stumbled the gypsy peddlar, the midwife, the schoolteacher, not to mention, under cover of night, the *andarte*, a guerrilla on a clandestine visit to his village at Eastertime, his hand full of red poppies. Millennia of activity. Who would go to her Rocky Mountains, her Canadian Shield, except in awe of rock?

Kostas was gone off on his project invoking the name of his people, leaving her to ask herself which was hers. How far back could she write the genealogy — three, four generations until there were no more names, only "souls" in the inventory of an absentee Polish landlord? Was this a people: serfs without lineage who knew only that they came from "here"? Were those her kinfolk labouring on the *kolkhoz* who had been abandoned to their separate and harrowing fate the day her grandmother had hoisted herself up on the wagon that would take her to the train that would take her to the ship that would land in Halifax? What then of the shore where *baba* landed, that grab bag of inheritances striving for a coherence called Canada? Her parents had been born there and now she: was she now sufficiently evacuated of Europe not to be disappointed with her homeplace but to have learned to love what was actually there?

He drove her out to the airport of Kalamata. It was early evening. The sun was slanting through the windshield of the car and gilding the dashboard. They didn't speak. He was playing a cassette. The song this time was about the students massacred by the guns on the tanks of the Junta during their sit-in at the Polytechnic in 1973, about how their martyred spirits come back to kiss the eyes of the sleeping. It made her cry. He abruptly ejected the cassette and gave it to her. In front of the terminal building they stood leaning against the car and holding hands. Then she picked up her bag and marched inside. He did not drive off right away but stood at the car's fender. She walked up to a window and looked out at him. They looked at each other. Then he opened the car door, gave her a salute with his clenched fist, got inside, and drove away.

— * —

*Did you think you would ever see him again?*
He had suggested that, in the event the socialists lost the election, he would leave Greece. He would come to see me in Canada en route for El Salvador.
*All that guerrilla training in Patras . . .*
He'd grown up in Xanthe, in the northeast, had spent hundreds of hours as a child scrambling through the hills in the company of his uncle, both of them with rifles, out hunting together. He told me that from his earliest memory there had been guns in his parents' house. His uncle had been in the Resistance. This is how he learned to hunt and shoot. This is how he learned to hate injus-

tice with an intensity of revulsion that made him puke. He told me some of that uncle's stories. How the guerrillas dressed themselves in whatever was at hand—old army uniforms, Italian uniforms, village sandals—and most carried Greek army rifles from the First World War, or no weapon at all. How starving children, rooting about in garbage, were recruited by German intelligence. How, near the end, neither side took prisoners. How in the main square of the town of Trikala, strung up on a gibbet, swung the head of the fiercest guerrilla of them all: Aris, betrayed, some say, by his own comrades.

*Did he want you with him in El Salvador?*

No. He spoke instead of how I could help the struggles of the Greek people for national self-determination. By writing about the truth of their history, the justice of their ideals, and so on.

*Did you feel up to the task?*

As long as he kept feeding me stories, I knew that I could do it. On that drive to Kalamata he told me the story of the Polytechnic. He was there, behind the barricaded, slogan-strewn gates when the tanks, manned by soldiers the students called brothers and topped by the pitiless searchlights, crashed through the gates at 3 AM. and crumpled them like matchsticks, the rest of the city asleep. And I felt ashamed. I did not know this story. Where the hell was I, and all my friends, on November 17, 1973, that this story should not be known? I felt cheated, as though, in a photo album, between the sequences from Paris in 1968 and Saigon in 1975, there was a blank page waiting for us to assemble the pictures: Greek students pressed against the gates of the Polytechnic and holding up a sign, WE WANT BOOKS! Dying in ambulances staffed by the secret police, buried in unmarked graves. . . . I found my datebook for 1973, by the way. Here's the entry for November 17: "Ceta's birthday party BYOB."

— * —

Of course he wouldn't be able to imagine her place. The light at midnight was still blue, the shadow was two porcupines eating saskatoon berries, the sounds were a ticking clock and a moth burning to death in the yellow flame of the kerosene lamp.

If he were here, she would take him to the patch of wild strawberry, crush the tiny, piquant fruit on his tongue, take him to where the orange tiger lilies grow in the ditch. Or look behind them, on the slope, the weathered wood of a small church, topped by a tarnished dome. It was empty and useless. The Galicians built it and then died. See here, under the wild buckwheat, their graves. Can you imagine this, Greek: bones in virgin soil?

She wanted her revenge on him. On that moment when he flipped out the cassette of Mikis Theodorakis and his bloody partisans and played Bob Dylan and said, "Now you tell me what this song is about." And she began, word by word,

*Well, I see you got your brand-new leopard-skin pill box hat*

but could not go on. Even in the broad May daylight as they rattled through the Peloponnese she felt spooked by the characters of all Kostas's stories: the ghosts of bellicose *klephtes* and assassinated politicians and partisans strung up from nooses, poets flayed alive and students with broken skulls, all shuffling their chains outside the car window.

*Well, you look so pretty in it*
*Honey, can I jump on it sometime?*

He was smirking. She wanted to say, Bob Dylan is an American. It's his American genius to present himself as a thing created out of the blue, as though the past were merely accumulated autobiography. She was not like that. She had a past. It was what she was looking for in the ancestral webbing that slings together the flaking Byzantine frescoes in a deserted church near Sparta with her *baba's* wedding dance outside the onion-domed church in Tulova.

Two could play this game. In a flurry of letters to Patras, poste restante, she pressed him with stories of her own. "You talk of Turks and Ottomans, bandits and guerrillas, wars of liberation and those betrayed. Well, I have heard these stories too, of Huns and Mongols and Cossacks, wars of genocide and treachery. Can you sort your story out from mine? You tell me of your parents' neighbour, a man the anti-Communists strung up on a lamp-post and left there to rot, and I tell you of my great-uncle Petro, dragged out of his hut at Christmastime and into the barn and shot by Ukrainian nationalist insurgents, and left to die face down in the dung for the crime of his Red Army uniform. And what of your brothers and sisters and their youth in the torture cells of the Security Police and of *my* generation, condemned to another death by the boredom of their enemies? Are we not related after all, Greek?"

In return he phoned her from time to time. She could hear the coins dropped in the box and imagined him under the thin light of the booth, surrounded by the pitch-black night of the road. It was after the election of the socialists that, on hearing his jubilant voice, she decided she would return to Greece. "Yes, come," he said. "We need you. You can help us."

He met her at the Athens airport and drove her straight to Nafplion where he helped her find a room. They stood on the balcony and, against the fading light, he suddenly burst into a kind of dance, skipping backward and forward, thrusting his right arm piston-like while the left hand rested on his hip. He had been a champion swordsman at the university in Thessaloniki, he explained, and these were the parries and thrusts of the Bavarian style. He seemed suddenly theatrical, and as though he were missing a cape.

Then he was gone. For the next two months it was like this: he would arrive unannounced at her room having driven like a maniac from (she supposed) Patras; they would make love and then go out to eat. Pulling shrimp apart and licking fingers, he informed her he had to go back to Patras because that night the head of the Communist Party would be speaking on television. She wondered why he couldn't watch this on television in Nafplion and stay the night with her. But she made no protest. She understood that in his own good time he would let her know what she had come here for.

— ∗ —

*It sounds like an anticlimactic reunion.*
He apologized but he simply didn't have much time for me. He was under tremendous strain, I could see that. Now that the socialists had been elected, he and his comrades expected the Americans to begin their behind-the-scenes manoeuvres. In any event, he promised me that in the New Year he would take me with him on his trips again.
*What about the fiancée?*
When I pressed him about this, he became angry. Said no, Fotini did not know about me. Said I was not to ask about her again.
*Did you feel he had to choose — her or you?*
No. It was enough to have some quiet moments of happiness between us. One night of a full moon, for instance, we went walking along the beach. We sat on an overturned fishing boat and told each other the names of the planets and constellations and quoted bits of poetry and confessed that neither of us knew much about the sea. Then a pregnant cat waddled into view and straight under Kostas's hand. As he stroked her, he said he liked cats because they were like women: one minute they are rubbing

up against you like you were the only one in the world they cared about; the next minute they are on their way, tail in the air, without a backward glance.

— * —

He was hiding her away. The lovers under the glare of the sun at the summertime beach had become the furtive couple embracing behind the shutters of hotel rooms as the winter light went out. He was all skin and bones, so slight it was like embracing a child. Her own body struggled for its satisfaction under his nonchalant, distracted hand.

The dark face, the once-broken nose, the clear brown eyes. Already under the skin she could see the face of the Old Man of the village, even though he said he expected to die violently before the age of forty.

She cursed the things that estranged them. Language, for instance. She always spoke carefully, picking the common words, but he would swear and slap his knee as he strained to find a word he did not have, and she could not help. She felt stupid before his language, he was enraged before hers. She showed him photographs from home. He stared at them without comprehension. He did not know how the earth could be flat or how black earth smelled. She showed him photographs of friends and tried again to explain the passions that bound them but, even as she spoke, of Ukrainian weddings and the crisis in the Writers' Union, of a picket line and a study group, she could see on his face how risible these were compared to the project of the Greek revolution. She put the photographs away and asked him to explain again the problem of Cyprus.

But she never stopped wanting heat in their embrace and harmony in their discourse. *Her* Greek ideals.

She was in a bar. It was cosy and polished and masculine. Was she going to grow up like one of those middle-aged ladies who sat alone in foreign bars and scribbled in a notebook to give them a reason to be there that way not whoring? In one ear, the chatter of a Greek conversation. In the other, a song on the phonograph. "Mack the Knife" by Louis Armstrong. Oh Bertolt, oh Brecht. Oh hell.

She saw Kostas one more time. Although it was a wet and blustery day, he insisted they walk along the seawalk. As they rounded the bend towards the open sea, a raging wall of wind and wave swept over them. They clung together until it retreated. Now soaked to the skin they returned to her room and laid his clothes to dry on the radiator. He would have to leave in an hour.

She had many things on her mind and she felt the press of time. She would begin to speak — both of her loneliness and of recent dramatic world events, especially in Poland — and he would turn away to look out the window or to light a cigarette. He poured out a brandy and ruffled through her newspapers. Finally, he wrapped her towel around himself, Roman senator style, stepped barefoot into her high-heeled shoes and strutted mockingly around the room, his flat, narrow buttocks swaying waggishly within the folds of the towel. At that moment, his hairy legs knock-kneed as he pivoted coyly at the window, she thought he was revolting. She yelled at him to sit down and burst into tears.

— * —

*Why so high strung?*
His hairy legs, one crossed over the other bargirl-style. I couldn't bear it. The stack of newspapers that didn't interest him. It was the end of December 1981. On December 13, the army in Poland had taken over in a coup d'état and crushed Solidarity, the independent labour movement. The revolution. That's what was in those news-

papers. I had been devastated by the news and felt very lonely.

*You had friends in Nafplion.*

The ones I cared about were back in Canada, huddled together, talking, analyzing, strategizing, while I was stranded in Greece, sitting in cafés with flickering TV sets. The foreign newspapers always arrived a day or two late. Every morning for two weeks I was in an agony of suspense knowing that whatever it was that I was reading had already been superseded by events that I would not know about for another twenty-four hours. So I watched grainy grey film of snowbound Warsaw, bulky figures flitting in and out of fog, in the television studio the clear, bland faces of the Army spokesman. I thought I would choke.

*So you were looking forward to talking with Comrade Kostas.*

When we were in my room together, drying off, I tried to tell him what I had gone through. Something of my feelings attached to Solidarity and those distressing events. Just, as before, we had sat close together, almost embracing, and shared our indignation and hurt in the recital of the events at the Polytechnic, so now I wanted us to share the events in Poland, the Silesian coalminers shot to death, the strikers herded into freezing prison camps, the students beaten like dogs. I was naive enough to believe that, as a man of the left, he would champion the Polish workers.

*Let you down, did he?*

He started yelling at me half in Greek that I was stupid, understood nothing. He shouted that Poland was a captive of the Roman Catholic church, hostage of the CIA and prey of counter-revolutionaries. He barked that the security of the Soviet Union was sacrosanct; that nothing must be permitted to jeopardize it, least of all a so-called workers' movement in a workers' state. Finally, with a look of contempt screwing up his face, he spat out out, "You are not a Communist!" And I knew I had failed him.

*Not to mention you weren't a Greek, or a fiancée.*

So I let him go. Or he left. My head was running other movies than his.

— ＊ —

Inside his head he saw ragged bands of desperate Communist guerrillas scrambling on the nude hills for shelter from the pulverizing bombs, saw a friend disappear into the back of a police van in the middle of the afternoon, saw the muzzle of a tank swing in his direction as he yelled a revolutionary slogan, saw a village—squat, stony huts on the slope of a hill bearing dusty olive trees—from which he led a bride in a white dress to the church of St. Nicholas.

He had promised her his country, he had promised her his stories, he had promised her the comrades she could help. Now this place was depopulated. Lies? Who could say? His stories brought her here, to a window from which she could see a red-tiled roof and a hibiscus tree blossoming in the rain. A ragged guerrilla passed by there all the same.

On New Year's Eve, she was preparing to go out with friends when she was summoned to the hotel telephone. In musical but apologetic tones, a woman's voice at the end of the line told her, "Excuse me, I am Fotini." Fotini went on to say that she was the wife of Kostas and the mother of their two children and that— she excused herself again—she had found certain letters in her husband's pockets. And that he would like to say something too. After a couple of seconds, Kostas himself came on the line to say, in a flat, uninflected voice, that he had told her many lies and would not see her again.

## — Who Is Kostas? —
## (A Probable Biography)

It is 1950 in Xanthe. Kostas is five years old. Dressed in Sunday best, he sits stiffly on a wooden chair in his parents' modest home and watches the celebrating adults. His uncle, who has just been demobilized from the army, is telling stories. He is a big hero and boasts of killing Communists. Noticing Kostas, he pulls the boy off the chair and onto his lap. "And this one," he shouts, clapping his big hand on the boy's shoulder, "this one will know what to do with those sons of whores!"

It is 1960. Kostas is in a movie theatre watching old swash-buckling films. In the hills, by himself, he picks up a long, straight stick and pretends he is Errol Flynn.

It is 1970. The Junta has been in power for three years. Kostas's uncle has got him a job in the post office in Thessaloniki. One afternoon, from the window of the room where he works, he sees a man he knows, someone he has gone to school with, being arrested. In broad daylight. The man, who had been walking across from the post office, is suddenly engulfed by two plain-clothesmen and frog-marched into the back of a van that is pulled up curbside. It is over in seconds. Kostas puts on his jacket and goes out for coffee. He chainsmokes five cigarettes.

It is November 1973. Kostas is in Athens to take his mother to a doctor. He has heard there is something going on at the Polytechnic. He walks in that direction. A block from his destination he sees a crowd running towards him. They are strangely quiet, although some have blood on their heads and faces. Kostas halts. Now come puffs of tear gas and he begins to cough violently. He looks at his watch, turns around, and hurries back to the doctor's office, his handkerchief covering his mouth.

It is 1980. Kostas lives in Patras in a small apartment with his wife, Fotini, a former post office employee, and their two children. The children's squalling drives him crazy. In the evenings after supper he goes to a neighbourhood *kafenion* to meet his buddies. They play cards and watch the soccer games on television. When a politician comes on the screen, they all jeer.

It is May 1981. Kostas is driving up a road to a mountain village. There is a foreign woman with him. They stop at the village square and get out, Kostas carrying his briefcase. There is a small group of farmers sitting around as if waiting for him. The woman sits on the edge of the group, stares at the scene a long while, then pulls a book out of her bag, begins reading. Kostas is speaking, arguing with the men, who seem unmoved. He opens the briefcase, takes out a handful of papers, distributes them. He gesticulates, shrugs. The men look at him. Kostas makes his pitch again.

He was selling agricultural chemicals manufactured by an American multinational corporation. She had seen the advertising flyers while rummaging for cassettes on the back seat of his car, but had refused to assimilate the information. She wanted a lover who was leafletting the Greek countryside with revolutionary pamphlets. As for Kostas, he wanted someone who would see him, see him in the blue hills back of Pylos, stride manfully into the village square.

He has a foreign woman on one arm, his briefcase tucked under the other. He leaves her at a table under a yellowing plane tree, then joins a group of villagers who are waiting quietly. He has been here before, has climbed out of his car, rumpled from the long, hot drive from Patras, sweaty and bored, belching little burps from his oily lunch. Now he stands in front of the men of the village, speaking. But he is thinking of the woman, and how she is watching him. He thinks of the men watching her watching him. He raises his voice, thumps a nearby table. He tells a joke. They laugh, shuffle in their chairs. He throws back his shoulders. The evening breeze lifts up the hair on his arms. He is seeing himself later, with the woman at his side in a shuttered room. Her hands are on his belt. Already he can taste her on his tongue.

# INSIDE THE COPPER
# MOUNTAIN

*A thunder of resurrection on the mountain*
*is being announced for me.*
*Smash your fists against despair,*
*hiding within the copper mountain.*

—Vasyl Stus

ecause I keep files about dissidents, especially those who were martyred in Soviet Ukraine, I cut his picture out. It was printed in a glossy English-language magazine, *Ukraine*, from Kiev, mailed faithfully to me for months though I had no subscription. It shows a close-cropped, dark-haired man of about forty, with big ears, a strong jaw, and a dark, bright and mettlesome gaze straight into the camera. He's wearing a black turtleneck sweater and looks to me like a Ukrainian Marlon Brando from *On the Waterfront*.

I pin this up on the bulletin board above my desk. It's one of those portraits in which the eyes follow you as you move around the room. He stares at me, I stare at him.

His name is Vasyl Stus. I know that he was a poet and a member of that band of young writers in Ukraine called the "Sixties people" whose first novels, first collections of poems, first screenplays blew their hot breath briefly in the 1960s in the thaw after the Terror and the War. I have never read his poetry, and am guilty, I suppose, of hallowing the singer not the song. I do not know what exactly he did that got him arrested. I do not know when this photograph was taken. Has he been to the camps yet? Or is he waiting for the van to pull up in the street below his flat in Kyiv?

I do know he died in the Zone in September 1985, somewhere inside that vast complex of penal colonies, prisons, and psychiatric hospitals where, until the late 1980s, the USSR held its political prisoners. "Why couldn't you have held on six more months?" I cry. "You would have been freed."

He's big-boned, broad-shouldered and robust, I guess years away from his death, with his fight still ahead of him.

I kiss my two fingers and lay them on his cheek.

*Thousands of miles away from your grave I will find you in my books, and I will drag you into my language, my purposes, and my memory. There in my memory is a Pantheon of lost loves, men who were heroes I wooed and lost. And you are going to be there with them.*

*You come from the green kingdom. I see you upright in the greenery, leaning on a thick stave stripped crudely of its branches, your round, dark head crowned with wild roses I have plucked from roadside ditches. I sit squinting in the noon hour sun. You haunt the shade.*

In the mid 1960s, I was a student of Russian literature, reading Russian dissident poets and collecting their books. I was not then aware of dissident Ukrainian poets who were not in any case at the centre of my concern.

My reading persisted and the books became a library. Then other books joined them, the excruciating stories of the men and women of the Gulag. Those who had the means to do so smuggled out their stories while still in the camps. Those who survived wrote their memoirs and smuggled them out of the USSR to the West where émigré foreign-language presses received them. Some were eventually translated. I would come across them gathering dust in piles of remaindered books or yellowing in second-hand bookshops, as though their content had proved too arcane for readers used to more ordinary worlds. And still the habit persisted, until the library became a harrowing archive of that archipelago of punishment called the Zone.

By this time I had become aware of the particularly relentless persecution of the Ukrainian intellectuals and in time set myself to learn the language of my grandparents so I could understand better who these dissidents had been and what had happened to them. I began subscribing to Ukrainian journals and magazines. I noticed the repetition of certain names, made connections among events, stared at photographs.

## — A Photo —

A patch of hummocky land, sprouting weeds and three small wooden posts. The caption: "Cemetery of unmarked graves along the Potma railway (Moscow-Kuibyshev line)." This line was laid by political prisoners and the graves belong to those who died building it. They have numbers but no names. The photograph was taken in 1976. There is no other information.

## — Short Course in the History of the Zone —

In 1921, near Arkhangelsk on the Barents Sea astride the Arctic Circle, the Soviet government set up the extermination camp, Kholmoger, for the purpose of physically destroying the political enemies of the Bolshevik Party.

In 1973, the Ukrainian, Baltic, Russian and Jewish inmates of Camp VS 389–35 in Perm region, where Vasyl Stus would serve his second term, marked the anniversary of the establishment of concentration camps in the USSR with a hunger strike and demanded that henceforth September 5 be known as the Day of Protest Against Persecution. They called themselves *zeks*, from "z.k.," Russian slang for "zakliuchennyi" (prisoner).

Prisoners worked on construction sites without proper work clothes and in unheated workshops with their bare hands unprotected from the frozen metal. They ate where they worked, with no washing facilities and no tables, and worked forty-eight hours a week.

One long-term political prisoner, Anatoly Marchenko, could remember exactly when he ate cucumbers: one in 1964 and a second in 1966.

## — Kyiv, September 4, 1965: The KGB Opens a File on the Poet —

There were several hundred packed into the *Ukraina* cinema in downtown Kyiv the day that the new Sergei Paradzhanov film, *Shadows of Forgotten Ancestors*, premiered. The word had gone around that "something was going to happen." After the screening, the journalist Viacheslav Chornovil and the critic Ivan Dziuba strode to the stage, grabbed the microphone and denounced the recent arrests of artists and intellectuals, their colleagues and friends, who had been protesting publicly the Russification of Ukrainian culture.

The plainclothes police in the audience did not let Dziuba finish speaking but switched on sirens to drown out his words and then chased him off the stage. Vasyl Stus, the writer of a handful of published poems, stood up from the floor and shouted out a challenge to the crowd: "All those against tyranny, rise up!" Only a few responded, here and there standing up and sticking their necks out.

I shake out the Gulag memoirs, the weird volumes of memorabilia published by Ukrainian exiles and émigrés in Munich and Baltimore, the collections of underground *samizdat*, and note how Stus's name, his dates, his first notoriety spill out from the footnotes.

And then, like a gift, in the magazine *Ukraina*, I find four dense pages of the memoirs of the critic Mykhailyna Kotsiubynska about her friend, Vasyl Stus: "In the Mirror of Memory," written June 1990.

"From time to time in recollections and dreams," she begins, "a blinding projected apparition appears before me like a magic eye in the hopeless nights."

I am enchanted. I haul out my Ukrainian-English dictionary. I look for words, following with my finger the elaborate syntax as the tender remembrance of this woman rises from the paper, a photographic image emerging from its developing bath. I do pages of this work before I realize, fascinated, that Mykhailyna's initials are the same as mine: MK. The temptation is huge: to enter her words here and join her voice contrapuntally as the woman who did not know Stus. But *she* did, and there I am, she is, beside Vasyl Stus in the *Ukraina* cinema in Kyiv. They are sitting together and fate, Vasyl's fate, is about to throw them into a friendship to the death.

— MK —

. . . we stood up together. He shouted out something despairing — "Whoever is against tyranny, stand up now!" — while trembling in every cell of his body. I could feel it through the arm I held around his shoulder as we left the hall.

"Poet," she wondered, "how are you going to manage to live in this world?"

Poet, how are you going to manage to live in this world? You are large and strong. Your voice fills whole rooms. I remember the morning you came to me in the garden, smiling with the pleasure of the lilacs and held out to me one thick, radiant stem that shook in your trembling hand.

You come from the green kingdom. I see you upright in the greenery, leaning on a thick stave stripped crudely of its branches, your round, dark head crowned with wild roses I have plucked from roadside ditches.

In the winter you come with your handful of seed, sowing in our households the new life latent in the wild grass. You bear the cranberry branch of your good wishes. "Good fortune to you," you whisper. "Sister." I light a candle, a solitary fire in the snowdrifts. If I look after you, if I watch you go, you will melt like beeswax.

A couple of weeks after his outburst at the cinema, Stus was expelled from his doctoral studies for "systematic violations of the norms of behaviour of graduate students and staff members of research institutions." A year later he was dismissed from his assistantship at the State Historic Archives: he had become unemployable in his profession.

Soviet Writer Publishing House returned his manuscripts without explanation and a collection of poems already slated for publication was purged from the schedule. He found employment as a labourer on the construction of Kyiv's subway line but was fired after a few months, in a Soviet Catch-22, for working outside his specialization. How did he survive? Under a pseudonym he published translations of Rilke and Goethe.

## — Roll Call of the Arrested: 1965 —

Accused of anti-Soviet propaganda and agitation and defended by Stus in his protest in the cinema: Ivan Rusyn, Valentyn Moroz, Mykhailo Osadchy, Mykhailo Horyn, Ivan Hel, Panas Zalyvakha,

Myroslava Zvarychevska, Anatoly Shevchuk, Ivan Svitlychny. They were respectively: a member of an amateur choir, a history teacher, a journalist, a philologist, a locksmith, a painter, a proof-reader, a linotypist, a critic. These names are just a sample.

Here is Vasyl Stus's poem to his arrested friend, Ivan Svitlychny, who was under intense pressure to confess:

> *Like a star he beams in from the gloom*
> *But he says nothing, nothing, nothing, nothing.*

Stus's friends were charged under Article 62, Section 1, of the Criminal Code of the USSR with "anti-Soviet agitation and propaganda designed to undermine or weaken Soviet power," were found guilty and sentenced to four, five, six years in forced labour camps in the Mordovian Autonomous Republic southwest of Moscow.

Only the KGB and the criminal justice system paid them official attention. Even the Ukrainian Soviet press made no mention. Friends of the accused, among them Stus, wrote a flurry of open letters and appeals on behalf of their associates, and stood outside the courtrooms demanding to be let in.

It does not seem like much, a signature on an appeal against "lawlessness," say. I suppose they never did stop being afraid, but they tried to act as though they were not and swallowed back the salt secreted by their own faint hearts.

Stus stood at courtroom doors of their trials demanding to be let in. Dissident Nadia Svitlychna was there with him. Interviewed twenty years later, she remembered how they had stood together in the square opposite the court house where one of the trials was going on. "Vasyl lit a cigarette. His hands were shaking." He was already suffering from the gastric ulcer that would torture him in the camps.

They milled about outside the bolted courtroom doors and threw flowers. At the trials of 1966 there were flowers everywhere. They fluttered down from the sky as the prisoners filed past the cordons of police on Pekarska Street in Lviv, carpeting the *via dolorosa* between the Black Marias and the drunken judges like a Carpathian meadow. "Hurrah! Hurrah! Hurrah!" the friends shouted, pelting the police with carnations. When the poet Lina Kostenko threw roses to her friends at the yawning courtroom doors, the police dropped to the ground as though she had lobbed a bomb. Red tulips stuck into the railings of the prisoner's dock were snatched away by shrieking prosecutors before their damage could be done.

Q: Did you know [Stus] personally? What was he like as a person?

A: Certain "snapshots" from my meetings with him are fixed in my memory.

Winter 1966: Nadia Svitlychna and the artist Alla Horska go to Vasyl's wedding. In the bureaucratized, conveyor-belt atmosphere of the state Palace of Happiness, they have come to add a little human warmth to the proceedings of the "registration of marriage." Vasyl comes up to Nadia and asks forgiveness. "For what? I don't know. He was taking my brother's arrest very badly," she tells the interviewer on Radio Liberty in 1985.

I imagine the bridegroom proud in a stiff black suit a little short in the leg, the bride grasping red carnations, her knees knocking under her skirt. Are they holding hands? Does he encourage her with his hand pressed against the small of her back? Nothing. There is no bride here at all. She has a name — Valentyna Popeliukh — but no figure, no face.

*Your house is orderly. The icon of the* Theotokos, *the Godbirthgiver, hangs discreetly in her alcove. A branch of pussywillow blesses our entry to the kitchen. Your furniture is pale, creased. This is very far away from the sweatshops of the Revolution. You are wearing suspenders. You smoke furiously while beating out the rhythm to the male duet from "The Pearl Fishers." Your wife sits curled up on the sofa and glares coldly at you. She has been looking at you like this for some time, while you and I have been* talking. She is thin and beautiful. Her neck is fluted with grooves. She does not wear the look of a woman in love. Perhaps I do.

He loved her. He chose her. He bedded her. Where is she? When I find the poems, I look for her as though I were rifling through her husband's pockets for his secrets.

> *And there will be parting enough for two,*
> *and there as well will be a silent joy —*
> *to feel with the whole heart the long debt*
> *owed to a past with a white headboard [...]*
> *and a pair of long arms, drunk upon the dark*
>
> —Vasyl Stus

It was sometime that same year, 1966, that Mykhailyna met Vasyl on Volodymyr Hill on her way to the district office of the Communist Party where, after a seven month long ordeal of extricating herself from Party membership, she was finally going to turn in her card.

— MK —

And here was Vasyl, waving his arms about, shouting cheerfully at me. He had just finished his translations of Lorca, and I can still hear how his voice broke when he came to the line "Cordoba, distant and alone."

*You are driving me back to the city, through a black tunnel of night crackling with the green ice of the cold. Suddenly, you slam on the brakes, pull over to the side of the road and scramble out of the car, crying "Look! Look!" It is the Aurora Borealis leaping all over the sky. You have unhunched your shoulders and are laughing. I move towards you and put my hands in your pockets and nuzzle my face in your thick coat;*

*you hold me, rocking back and forth. I can hear the snow sqeak under
your heels.*

*Later you will say that we sought each other out. But you are wrong. In
the rooms where we gathered, you were telling us that the comrades' position on Afghanistan had driven you to despair. I was listening. But I was also
lusting after you, admiring the trim set of your hips bound in a narrow,
leather belt, the heft of your shoulders under the cotton shirt that gaped
open at your throat (you fiddled with the top button and I imagined you
opening your shirt for me, button by button, a little strip-tease unwrapping
your soft-furred chest contoured perfectly for my fingertips, my cheek, my
lips closing in on your left nipple.*

In 1970 a collection of Stus's poems, *Zymovi Dereva* (*Winter Trees*),
was published by an émigré press in Brussels. Vasyl wrote to
Vira Vovk, a Ukrainian-Brazilian poet who had visited Ukraine
in the 1960s, that he was developing a "kind of obliviousness."
He was content, he said. He strung up a hammock under the
pines, poured himself a glass of whiskey, looked up at the sky.
"My wife's at work, my son's in daycare, I write, I relax." It's
an image I will come across again, in a poem from the cycle
"Through Oblivion." "The wife is at her job/The son is in daycare/
Silence/Enjoy yourself/Until the hour peaks/Sit. Rejoice." I do
not begrudge the poet his domestication. All hell is about to
break loose.

In November 1970, Alla Horska, a good friend who had been
at Stus's wedding, is found dead, her friends assume murdered,
in the cellar of her father-in-law's house outside Kyiv. It is Nadia
Svitlychna, dragging the local militia with her to the cellar door,
who finds her. No relative or friend is allowed to examine the
body; the coffin remains sealed.

The friends stand at the open grave in a vacant lot outside the
city, holding each other against the December wind. On the
anniversary of her death in the years to come the circle will be
smaller—the friends sense this already. Vasyl reads his poem in

Alla's memory: "For we are very few. We are a pinch of earthly salt . . ."

A year later Stus is arrested in a storm of arrests known as the General Pogrom, the harshest single assault by the KGB on dissidents in Ukraine since the death of Stalin. The KGB did not limit its sweep to political dissidents or "conspirators" or "gutterpress profiteers." Virtually an entire generation of writers and artists was repressed.

Sympathizers found themselves threatened with dismissal from work, watched helpless as investigators removed their books from their incriminating libraries and the police ransacked their houses. Their family members were hauled along with them for interrogation, and, as witnesses at their friends' trials, they were remorselessly bullied and humiliated in cross-examinations of breath-taking vulgarity.

Radio Peking, 1969: "The Soviet revisionist renegade clique has transformed the first socialist state into a great fascist prison."

The pogrom peaked in January, 1972. Hundreds would be imprisoned, among them many who had already done terms in prison and camp after the crackdown of 1965–66.

Here they went again. Valentyn Moroz, the history teacher. Ivan Hel, the locksmith. Mykhailo Osadchy, the journalist. Mykhailo Horyn, the philologist. And some debutants: Viacheslav Chornovil, Ivan Dziuba, Iryna Kalynets, Yevhen Sverstiuk, Leonid Pliushch, Ivan Svitlychny. And Vasyl Stus.

> It would be naive to believe
> that among the five thousand who perished
> while building Cheops' pyramid
> there was no poet.

> —Mykola Horbal,
> "Parts of an Hourglass"

On January 12, 1972, while Stus was in western Ukraine being treated for his gastric ulcer, the KGB ransacked his apartment and, next day, issued a warrant for his arrest on charges of involvement in an espionage ring. When they returned to his apartment a month later it was to confiscate his library (Pasternak, Gorky, Solzhenitsyn, Marx, Jung, Lorca) and virtually everything he had written in the last fifteen years: poems, essays, translations, and his one and only published collection of poetry, *Winter Trees*, published abroad.

Meanwhile he was arrested, held in prison, and interrogated. According to notes that were smuggled out of the Zone during his first imprisonment, he accused his interrogators of acting like "Stalinist dogs." He was taken forcibly to a psychiatric hospital, dragged down through the hallway of the interrogation isolator in Kyiv, kicking, and screaming to the prisoners in their cells that "They are taking Vasyl Stus to the Pavlov Insane Asylum!" When Mykhailyna and her friends accidentally learned of this, their alarm and anxiety increased a hundred-fold.

Stus was finally put on trial August 31, 1972, in Kyiv Regional Court under revised charges of slandering the state. He was found guilty, and on September 7 sentenced to five years in special regime labour camp in Mordovian ASSR and three years internal exile. Oddly, in spite of his own sustained activity since 1966 on behalf of colleagues in jail and on trial, I come across no material describing efforts mounted in his defence by others nor any eye-witness account of his trial. Only a plaintive bewildered little note struck by Mykhailyvna: that although she was to be summoned and questioned as a witness in other friends' trials, she was never summoned to Vasyl's—and all these years later it is as if she regrets that she had not been put to the test.

His [Stus's] arrest would not be totally unexpected, of course. In fact, there was a certain logic in this barbaric act, a natural continuation of those ideological "witches' sabbaths" that had been gathering momentum. Judicial persecution for heresy became our reality.

They were forced to live in it and for all of 1972 they lived for news from There.

You called last night—I surprised as always to hear your voice, never quite expecting you to act the lover. But, then, may not friends call? You did not sound yourself; you were lonely, you said.

Listen to you: you miss me. You say you are surprised by the images intense nostalgia conjures up—lying together on the sofa, curled around each other, listening to music and chatting domestically, stroking each other (pulling items of clothing loose from belts to get at the unveiled flesh), leaving kisses sticky with Greek brandy.

You have no homesickness for love-making. You slide from my bed to wash, for it is time for you to go home. Ah, the marriage bed. And do you find your ardour there at three o'clock in the morning?

You said, if you had another life to live, you'd live it in one of the monasteries on Mount Athos. And where does that leave your lovers—standing on the Aegean shore waving good-bye at your little boat setting sail for the village of men?

I dream instead of the heat of the Peloponnese and stretching you naked on the rocks of Sparta. You swoon in the buzz of the honey bees and the speeches you would make dissolve in the back of your throat as my breast falls in your mouth. You cannot move. You are arched over the slope of the rock and I stroke your flanks with my hair. You make a sound like a little pup and spill into the cup of my hand. You sleep. I am awake. If you try to leave, I will know.

## — The Political Economy
## of the Zone —

The caption reads: "A rare photograph of a concentration camp watchtower deep in the forests of the Mordovian ASSR ." I don't know how they can be so sure. I see an indistinct patch of a forest and a wooden tower trellised like the fire watchtowers in national parks. There's a man up there, lounging on the railing. I suppose he's in uniform but I see no gun.

Mordovian ASSR, southeast of Moscow, west of the Volga, had been a dumping ground for political prisoners since 1917 when camp labour was used to build a highway and railway, the so-called Dubrovlag route. In 1980 there were eight camps on the route (including Stus's Number 19), holding between five hundred and twenty-five hundred prisoners each, and seven of them were special regime. On limited rations prisoners were pressed into labour in logging, lumbering, furniture-making, production of steering wheels and automobile chassis, glass-grinding, and the manufacture of souvenir cuckoo clocks for export.

I do not know what Stus laboured at. What I learn is that, even in camp, he kept up a barrage of verbal attacks on the KGB, compiling documents that he eventually was able to smuggle out of the camp and which, by 1975, were circulating in the west. The most famous was his own "J'accuse," published in a Ukrainian-language journal in New York in January 1976:

"I deem the KGB a parasitic, exploitative, and pernicious organization, on whose conscience lie millions upon millions of souls, shot, tortured, and starved to death. . . . I accuse the KGB of being openly chauvinistic and anti-Ukrainian because it deprived my people of word and voice. . . . I am sure that sooner or later the KGB will be judged as a criminal organization, openly hostile to the nation. I am not sure that I will live to see this judgement passed on it. Therefore, I beseech those who will judge this criminal organization to include my testimony and my accusations into the many volumes of its dossier. . . ."

He was writing to friends too. Mykhailyna heard from him, messages included in letters to his wife and coming under the "severe constraints" of the camp rules, when they arrived at all. "It was 1972," she recalls. "We lived for news from There."

She made a point of posting her letters from different cities, to "compensate" him for the sudden forcible withdrawal from "normal, live impressions." At other times she wrote him a kind of journal, exposing to him her interior, poetic landscape as though they were meeting (as they had done?) late at night after a concert, a play, and reviewing their particular pleasures. She goes to a Bach concert, she sits down to write Vasyl, "about music and spirituality, about the eternal and unchanging, about beauty and tragedy," wanting to recreate for him her "soaring of the spirit." It is as if the ache of his absence can be assuaged by confession ("the lofty tremulousness of my soul") but she says this letter was never received at his end.

*The silence is absolute. The clock sounds like a bomb winding up. I am lonely for you. Outside I know the tiny white honey-sweet blossoms of the saskatoon are changing slowly into berry fruit. If you were here, I would lay some on the pillow by your head so you would fall asleep with honey in your mouth.*

*Just so, as I lie in the cabin's bed, I have a slant view out the south window through to the burnished poplar trees and the piercingly blue sky that they are splayed across. I thought of your son the other day. He is taller than you now, he has the shadow of a moustache on his upper lip, and his voice is deepening.*

*Does he remember his childish sleep on this very bed, tucked in for a nap while you and I lay in the long yellow grasses by the overturned earth of the field? Did he wake up and look for you through the open window? Do you remember the blanket laid imperfectly over the dry stubble, the grasshoppers nibbling at the shoots of oats, the breeze bearing away our heat?*

# — Martyrology —

In July 1975 Stus was severely beaten by a non-political prisoner and sent to the camp infirmary to recover. As a matter of course, he was refused the medication for his perforated ulcer that, a month later, provoked an internal haemorrhage. He came very close to dying but not, as he had feared, alone. Boris Penson, fellow *zek*, was there. Here is what he wrote:

"I remember the date so well because the camp's loudspeaker system was transmitting the broadcast of the signing ceremonies of the Helsinki Accords. Just imagine: the solemn voice of [the newscaster] intoning about maintaining the respect for human rights to the fullest, and in the middle of the barrack lies Stus, all covered with blood. He had fainted and fell down; blood was everywhere and Vasyl was dying. Some three hours later two camp trustees come accompanied by four guards armed with automatics and leading two attack dogs. The trustees . . . carried him . . . some three hundred yards to the infirmary. . . . The hemorrhage was stopped and later the chief surgeon would brag to me that he pulled Stus out of the morgue."

Stus could not know that, at the other end of the Dubrovlag route, five women political prisoners, including Nadia Svitlychna, having heard Stus was bleeding to death, announced a hunger strike to protest the official maltreatment and offered to donate their own blood. They were shut up in the camp hospital and ignored.

In December 1976 Stus was taken to a prison hospital in Leningrad where three-quarters of his stomach was removed. Two months later he was back in the camp and promptly joined a fellow prisoner's protest against confiscation of mail. He was punished with cancellation of his special post-surgical diet.

Naked body searches. Enforced isolation. Solitary confinement in the freezing cold. Confiscated letters. The burning of several hundred poems found in a camp search. Reduced rations.

Stus went on hunger strike in defence of political prisoner Stefania Shabatura and her right to keep her drawings. Fellow *zeks* went on strike for Stus and his right to his poems.

Sergei Soldatov, who arrived a prisoner in 1976, called him Hetman (Cossack chieftain) "because I pictured him on a frisky, raven-black horse, in a gold helmet with a glittering sword in hand, at the head of a brave regiment of Cossacks going into battle." The Hetman would wait until everyone in the barrack was asleep (except for the insomniac, Soldatov) to creep out into the corridor and expel the groans he suppressed all day in his degenerating body.

And he still loved his bride.

## — Mikhail Heifetz Remembers 1976 —

"I had to convince my wife that, when she got to Moscow, she should make an appearance in the dissident circles and tell them about the confiscation of [Stus's] poetry. . . . My wife wasn't exactly a political person. But I could tell that she had practically drunk Stus's poems. Then she asked me a question, one which I'll never forget, so originally did it resonate in this politicized business:

> 'Are the poems dedicated to his wife?'
> Yes.'
> Then for him I'll do everything. Wherever it is necessary for me to go, I'll go.'"

Your women, Vasya! We are all possessed.

## — In The Poet's Own Voice —

Suddenly a whole new set of materials arrives across my desk: all the surviving writings of Vasyl Stus from the Zone. They have been published here and there in Ukrainian-language journals in the West since 1983, the year when his camp notebook "miraculously" made its way abroad (there are no details, only references to "indirect routes"), and now a researcher has brought them to me. There are also a few letters.

Abashed it has taken me so long to get to him, I open my dictionary and try to let the poet through. Finally, he is speaking for himself and he sounds vigorous in his outrage, even proud, as his manifestos and outcries fly from my ballpoint pen. But then suddenly he disappears into words I can't find in the dictionary or behind his inflexible righteousness. He is a man who will be broken before he will bend.

At the beginning of 1977 Stus began his three-year term of exile in a compound near Kolyma in eastern Siberia where he was assigned to forced labour in a gold mine, whose infrastructure had been laid down by slave labour in the 1930s. After a cursory examination by doctors he was pronounced "fit" and sent off to the Matrosov pit.

From his camp notebook:

"My work began. It was a Communist shock brigade. Half the workers were Party members. A model brigade. They were to educate me. There was a horrible dust at the mine-face because there was no ventilation: they were drilling blind vertical shafts. The hammer weighed close to fifty kilograms, the drilling rod, eighty-six kilos. We had to shovel out by hand after the drilling. The respirator (a cloth face mask we tied around our heads) was useless after half an hour—damp and covered with a layer of dust. So you throw it away and work without protection. They say that young men, right out of army service, become sick with silicosis after six months of this hellish work.

"Once I refused to work because there were no respirators. They promised to get me one. I said loudly that that wasn't the point: a respirator is a necessary protection for *every* miner. I asserted this general principle and protested against the violation of technical norms. So they found the respirators . . . and punished me for 'striking.'"

In some respects, life in exile was worse than in camp. According to Mykhailyna, "he felt completely solitary yet was never given the chance to be alone." It was against the regulations to live anywhere but in an assigned dormitory and for room-mates he had a group of rowdy, vodka-soaked drunks at least one of whom was a KGB informant. He feared ceaselessly for his papers and books and was forever at war with the KGB for his mail: "Dozens and dozens of letters simply disappeared. To my accusations they replied in a novel way: the mail bag at the Magadan airport terminal was full of holes! I sent telegrams to KGB chief [Yuri] Andropov: 'Your Service is stealing my mail.' There was no point."

He shattered his heels in a fall and hobbled for weeks on plaster casts, wobbling on crutches over ice and snow to the outdoor privy and, deprived of medicine, tried to heal himself with homemade solutions in which he soaked his gnarled feet. To top it off, a local newspaper, *Leninist Flag*, ran an article, "Friends and Enemies of Vasyl Stus," lavishly spread out over two issues, in which a local nurse testified that "Stus is prepared to rape and murder. He's similar to a fascist." Predictably, dozens of honest Soviet citizens wrote to the paper to register their outrage that such a pervert lived among them.

"He had nowhere to stretch out his soul," Mykhailyna writes. "'And you couldn't bear it. And you could never get warm.' So begins one of his Kolyma poems."

In the summer of 1978 Stus received word that his father was dying in Donbas. Refused permission to travel, he posted a notice on his dormitory door: "Do not disturb. On hunger strike for permission to bury my father." They let him go, accompanied the whole way to Ukraine by a "detachment of spies from the KGB."

"We buried father," he writes, "and I returned to Kolyma as if to prison." A cryptic statement, to say the least. He leaves out the fact that friends, whom he had not seen for six years, had come to the funeral to be with him, among them Mykhailyna, who in turn fails to mention Vasyl's wife who had come with their son. Had they all become already a little insubstantial, blurred by the unreality of everyday life beyond the Zone, so that the only real adventure was back at the Matrosov pit? But these are Mykhailyna's memories, and if she and her beloved friend sit alone under the fruit trees in a swoon of communion, I do not protest. They met the day after the funeral in his childhood home.

— MK —

It was a squat white house with a narrow porch and a table had been set up in the small garden under a tree. We sat at the table. "And it is you, you, my dearest friends. . . ." An aching feeling of happiness from the visit. Vasyl was very stoic and didn't say much, certainly no complaints or grievances. Reserved. There was pain and anxiety in him but not for himself.

Perhaps for his mother, withered by grief, stunned as much by the return of her son "from There" as by the death of her husband. Or for Mykhailyna with whom he walked among the mine tailings—so exotic for her!—away from all the watchful eyes at every doorway in the village, alone, not saying much, carrying their silence together.

*When you stood up to embrace me, I could see over your shoulder the thick, soft, grey sky. Everything was soft on the coast. I stood within two scenarios: in one, your arms were pressing me to your breast, your mouth* was on my neck, your heart thudding; in the other, trees were suspended in a grey cloud and whales shuddered within the cold bowl of the grey sea. Your hair tickled my cheek. Outside, red cedars bled decadent into the soil. Inside, an empty bottle of brandy, the tv guide, snapshots of your son. So, the Wife was fecund and child-bearing. I would bear books.

I put the two of you in scenes I imagine—let us say from a Gulag memoir, the scene of your last day among us. You are a provincial apparatchik getting ready for work. You brush the breadcrumbs off your lapel, check the contents of your briefcase for the fountain pen, explain that you will be detained this evening at a committee meeting. Your wife is distracted, thinking of the day ahead for herself—the grocery shopping, the Party wives' gossip, the half-completed translation of the Russian novel piled by her typewriter.

You are about to walk out of the house and into the void. Neither of you sees the dark car waiting outside the apartment courtyard. You peck your wife on the cheek and shut the door behind you. You are erased.

Later your wife will drive herself mad remembering that, on your last night together, she was too tired for love-making.

This scene has nothing to do with me.


— A Photo —

The last known photograph of Stus was taken in 1979 towards the end of his exile in Kolyma, though he would live another six years. You cannot see his eyes; they have sunk into the black shadows of his eye sockets. He holds his right arm bent awkwardly at the elbow as though it had been broken and never straightened out. He is wearing a heavy jacket. His head is tilted down ever so slightly but just enough to suggest, for the first time in any of his pictures, that he has been cast down and discouraged. For the first time I find it believable that he is a man who will die.

Completing his term in exile, Vasyl Stus returned to Kyiv in October 1979. Loath to ask anything of anybody, he made his own arrangements at the Paris Commune factory where he worked pouring molten metal into cast iron moulds, but he could barely walk, his feet hurt so. He next found work on the assembly line of a shoe factory, spreading glue on the soles of men's shoes.

— MK —

Those seven months before his second arrest that Vasyl lived in so-called freedom Mykhailyna remembers as "sombre, monotonous, and melancholy. It was hard for him to breathe in that suffocating atmosphere of the half-truth and the false, it was hard to meet former colleagues and acquaintances who would shake hands with him seemingly sincerely, all the while looking nervously about."

She, along with all the others, needed to keep a job, the money coming in, felt the distraction of family illnesses, food shortages, hard-to-get train tickets. They were all, she said, victims of the false and unfree.

*Once upon a time we did not like to leave each other. Now we dance chastely under the gaze of our friends, who separate us and we do not touch again until the party is finished and I, leaning against the wall, seated with my left leg crossed over my right knee, feel your fingers on my ankle. "Good night," you salute a little wearily, and you sweep out the door into the snow while I lean back against the wall, feeling the branding-iron of your fingers still hot on the bone of my ankle, and will myself to be still. I have no business to transact with you in the middle of the night. Such business is illicit, and you and I live in the light of day.*

## — The End Begins —

While still in exile, Stus wrote to the Ukrainian Helsinki Monitoring Group, an illegal watchdog organization that monitored the USSR's compliance with the Helsinki Accords on human and civil rights signed in 1973. Stus stated he wished to become a member.

For its monumental task, the Group had thirty-seven declared members. (The number of undeclared members was never disclosed.)

Stus must have understood that for a newly released political prisoner to engage politically in such a public manner was to invite immediate harassment and even repression. A particularly odious form of intimidation was being employed at that time: the fabrication of nasty criminal charges against former political prisoners who had just been released or were about to finish their term. By accusing them of rape, dope-dealing, and hooliganism, the authorities were able to throw them straight back into prison.

"Vasyl wanted to render his friends some real assistance, but what?" Mykhailyna wondered, having visited Stus with the news about a fabricated case against Viacheslav Chornovil. He heard her out, then withdrew from a drawer the pitiable savings from his labour in the pits and handed them over as a gift to Chornovil's wife who was getting ready, continues Mykhailyna, "to make the purgatorial trip to Yakutsk [ten thousand miles east of Moscow] where this shameful farce was being played out."

Yet there begins to coalesce around his "persona" a mystique if not a romance of the inevitability of his doom. Mykhailyna, so impressed by the inner person "unriddled by fear," understands that his refusal to erect the normal protective barriers necessary for the citizen in a police state will be his undoing. "He couldn't have lasted in our world. It was as though he had bared his chest to the gun."

In his notebooks, Stus mulls this over. And accepts that, even as he goes about the melancholy business of the free man at the factory and at home, out in the Zone the camp gates are already opening for his re-entry: "You don't choose fate. You accept it, as it presents itself."

October 1983, Amnesty International in London received a first-hand description from within the camps of life in the Special Regime Camp VS-389-36/1 near Perm, twelve hundred kilometres east of Moscow near the Ural Mountains, where Stus was being held. The report was written in Russian. Its author is not known:

"The regime in the camp is like that in a KGB investigation and isolation cell. . . . There is no ventilation and so it stinks. . . . The work cells are dark: electric light is necessary by day. . . . The light burns at night too. . . . In autumn and winter the electric light is very weak and flickers. . . . The privileges provided for by the Labour Code for the sick and disabled are not applied here. [Prisoners] must work to the death. [In 1980 their daily task was to fit cables to seven hundred electric irons. Most could manage only four hundred.] . . . The food is bad . . . groats, meat (a piece of gristle, bone) which is often rotten. We hardly ever get vegetables. . . . The water is very bad. Sometimes they bring drinking water into the kitchen, but most frequently there is none—and then they boil stagnant water, which is very dirty . . . it stinks but you have to drink it."

On May 14, 1980, seven months after his return to Kyiv, the KGB visited Stus at his workplace. That night he was served with a warrant for his arrest as a repeat offender against Article 62 of the Soviet penal code: "anti-Soviet agitation and propaganda designed to undermine or weaken Soviet power." He was interrogated, tortured, and sent to trial—his fate fulfilled.

At his trial in Kyiv he tried to speak in his own defence, was expelled from the courtroom and sentenced as an "especially dangerous recidivist" to ten years' forced labour and five years' internal exile.

The trial took place at the end of September 1980, in the hall

of the regional court packed with a specially verified and pre-
pared public brought in to give the appearance of an open trial.
No acquaintance, friend, or family member was admitted. But
Mykhailyna had been summoned to testify.

Vasyl was very thin and pale and rose to greet her but, as this
was not allowed, was made to sit down again. When it was her
turn to testify, she stood at the dock, her back to Vasyl so that she
kept trying to turn around to face him, for which she was repri-
manded by the Court. Asked to "describe Vasyl's personality,"
she rose to the occasion, her first public statement about Vasyl,
and went on to speak of him as she would years later, at memorial meetings.

— MK —

I spoke of him as a person of elevated conscience, a person of
honour and idea such as one meets very rarely in life. One should
applaud such a person, not put him on trial! I thanked Fate for
granting me the chance to know such a person; I said I tried to
be like him. Protest against lies and injustice was the only means
of existence for him.

As I left the courtroom, I glanced at Vasyl. He sat white-faced
and strained, clenching his fists. I never saw him again.

Half a moon hangs in the sky tonight. I stand inside its wan light and await
your return. You belong on my white pillows, your limbs smeared with candle glow. I am humming at the base of my tongue the love song that I have
swallowed. It is like a fruit whose yellow flesh I suck to slake the anguish of
your absence.

# — Camp Correspondence: An Archive of Letters —

In his novel *Cataract*, former *zek* Mykhailo Osadchy usefully reminds us that "*zeks* are not doomed creatures. They may write letters," one every fortnight. As with all Soviet literature, of course, the letters are censored. "A *zek* is supposed to write: 'Dear Mother (Sister, Wife): I have received your letter. I am living well. The administration is pleased with my work. I am involved in socially useful labor at the camp. . . . Yours with love.'"

"I wrote you a week ago but they confiscated the letter," writes Stus to his wife and son on March 22, 1982. "I shall try a second one. I got your package. For the third time they've cancelled one of your visits. So I don't know if we'll be seeing each other soon. I get no letters except yours. This is almost a rule. . . . How is the Kyivan Spring?"

A month later he asks for ballpoint pens even though every scrap of poetry he writes down, in hasty and diminutive script, is confiscated and he wonders whether he has already written all the poetry he is going to write.

August 8, 1982: "I got your letter of the 12th. You would have heard from me at the beginning of the month but they confiscated the letter. It had translations of Rilke in it (I guess they stuck in somebody's craw)."

In place of his rhymes he shouts obscenities at the "fascists and Gestapo agents" of the KGB. His stirring manifestos fall on deaf ears: the *zeks* are exhausted and the one who wrote a protest letter "to the authorities" has been thrown into solitary for a year.

"We have lost every right to belong to ourselves." He belongs to no one else either. The lines to his darlings are broken, his friends are cleaning toilets, his country is standing in a queue, hoping for bread. He holds the debris of his life's portion in his cold, grubby fingers and knows "you must create yourself from your own burning heart."

Stus writes to his son October 10, 1982: "If you have a clean, innocent heart, then you will live easily in the world, and you will know no evil. For you will be like a bright little fire, a pure beam, to whom all will be drawn with the purest of impulses. For you will be the finest person—like your mother and Baba Ilynka. Do not sin, my son. This is the first rule. Maybe the only one."

## — Death Watch: Anonymous Testimony published in Suchasnist —

"The last time I saw Stus was in 1981, in the Urals. He was going to the bathhouse and he stopped for a few minutes to look out at the taiga. He looked with the eyes of a poet, of a profound spirit as though he had absorbed into himself that which not everyone is given to see. His eyes, face, figure expressed withdrawal from the real order of things. He lived in another world entirely, inaccessible and incomprehensible not only to his jailors but to retribution too."

It has been said of prisoners in the Gulag that the experience of living in extreme deprivation is transformative: the sufferer becomes aware of the demands of an "internal voice" which calls the individual to sacrifice the body in order to save the soul. This is called a mystical experience and is perhaps the message of all Gulag literature, all reports from the "other side": the metamorphosis of the terror of imminent death into a feast for the spirit.

And now something rather extraordinary begins to happen: at the same point where the mortal Stus is brought low in physical anguish and humiliation (those body searches upon his squatting nakedness), those who were around him begin describing him as "spiritually refined," "tender," even "delicate," as though he were being transfigured before their eyes. He recited Rilke. He cited Plato and Seneca.

All around him are the weaker ones, who stammer and have bad dreams, who long to be drawn up into his field of energy and be electrified there. But they are in awe of him too, for he contains within the cellular structures of his passion a dense and nuclear loneliness.

In the final years, very few documents arrive from Camp 36-1 and no poems at all. His creativity, which may be divided into three periods, Pre-Camp, Camp, and Farewell, now lodges in his last three hundred poems which, collected as *Bird of Spirit*, never emerged from the camp. He is said to have written a good-bye to his mother, wife, sister, son, and friends in the Fall of 1984, but I have not found it.

In 1985, some time after Stus's death, exiled members of the Ukrainian Helsinki Group based in Washington, DC will send a notice to the Commission on Human Rights at the United Nations, to Amnesty International, and to International PEN noting that "all information about Stus, especially in 1984, [had been] extremely troubling." For five years his family had received no permission to see him, even when his wife, Valentyna Popeliukh, and his sister, Maria Stus, managed the two thousand kilometre journey to the camp. Meanwhile, the executive of the Ukrainian Writers' Union had cynically broadcast that "actually, V. Stus is well" and unpardonably went on to call him a "traitor, terrorist and murderer."

— "You aren't really here, not really here." —

For the entire last year, Stus was held in an isolation cell on reduced rations in spite of exhibiting dangerous symptoms of kidney malfunction.

He died on September 4, 1985 (precisely twenty years, to the day, after his heady protest in the Kyiv cinema), while working the night shift of a forced labour detail. This is one version. In another, he was on hunger strike.

All his writings remained the property of the KGB.

His family asked to bring home his body. The camp authorities refused. Because he had died before his term was up, they explained, he could not be removed from camp until he had "served" his entire sentence.

They dug the hole and laid him in it, buried under marker number nine in the camp cemetery. The marker was a wooden stake, and, according to the photograph in the newspaper I clipped out, someone has tied an embroidered cloth around it.

> *All the same there is nothing sweeter*
> *than this lost and indolent*
> *than this carefree, repellent, than*
> *this earth.*

— Vasyl Stus

## — The Film —

In 1989 Stanislav Chernilevsky decides to make a film: "In August 1989, I went to Chusiv [near the Perm camps] to organize the filming of the reburial of Stus's remains but the authorities told us he could only be reburied in winter — danger of epidemic, they said. We figured that sooner or later there was going to be a reburial and we'd better be prepared so we got a Konbas camera and three hundred metres of film stock and set off.

"From the 29th of August to September 1, we filmed the former establishment . . . where . . . Vasyl Stus had died. Our guide was Vasyl Ovsienko — he had been twice imprisoned with Stus.

"I got my first shock at the sight of the Zone when Ovsienko led us through the entry gates and I saw the tracks, now over-grown with weeds, down which thousands of people had shuf-fled, hands behind their back, day after day, year after year, with-out rest.

"He took us from room to room, told us who had been kept where, who died where. Stus died in cell number three. . . ."

I'm looking at their film, a tenth-generation video lent me by a col-league in Toronto, in the company of a friend whose grasp of the Ukrainian language is strong enough to catch the drift of this washed-out, wobbly version. The crew's inside one of the bar-racks, filming the plank beds and the inscriptions of the prisoners on the boards—"Murderers! Blood-suckers! Torturers!"—while Ovsienko tells them about Vasyl's last day of life, how he had been sent to the isolator cell and, going in, had said to a fellow prisoner, "I'm declaring a hunger strike to the end," and kept his word.

The film crew tramps around the deserted barracks, tripping over junk in the long grass. Ovsienko hoists himself up on the sill of a barred window to look inside "where Vasyl died." He ges-tures at the shutters that hang akimbo, the rusted bars, the eter-nal gloom of the cell. The camera follows him inside (there is a great deal of clattering sound including the roar of a second cam-era) and he demonstrates that the barracks rooms were as wide as a man with his arms outstretched.

Now we are at Room 12, where Stus sat before being hauled to the isolator. It faced north and never had the sun. On the night of September 4th, 1985, Ovsienko heard the sinister voice of one of the wardens hissing orders and then the noise of a body being dragged away "by thieves in the night."

The camp graveyard, surrounded tentatively by ramshackle fencing, is woolly and thorny like a prairie boneyard. Stus lies under a bed of wildflowers long gone to seed. The crew pokes around in the weeds and comes up with a shredded cloth and the remains of a small blue-and-yellow flag. They clear the grave, tie a new embroidered cloth around the grave stump, and light thin white candles.

In November 1989, Vasyl's son, Dmytro, a Kyiv University student, is finally given permission to unearth his father's remains. Standing in underground water, he digs with a pickaxe in the Ural earth. Carefully removing the rotting planks, he lifts up the blackened body in its shreds of camp uniform and lays it in its new coffin. There is a short prayer service at the open grave, the mourners masking their faces from the sulphurous air.

Later, Stus's mother will complain to a journalist: "An impressive delegation—two busloads—visited me. They bore portraits of Stus, flowers, wreaths trailing ribbons inscribed with phoney declarations: 'O Mother of the Martyr!' 'Hail Mother of the Famous Poet!' But I didn't want any of this. What I wanted was my own living son. I had lost three children: a daughter to famine, an older son to the mines and now this younger one to the Zone. I told them that I spoke now only with myself and the Scriptures."

And so, in 1989, the poet comes home.

At Boryspil Airport in Kyiv, in a cold winter's wind, some hundreds of ordinary people stood in a concentrated silence, holding Ukrainian flags and church banners, staring at the doors of the Baggage Department building. The Perm-Novosibirsk-Kyiv flight had landed an hour earlier.

Presently, a baggage car drove up and deposited three long packs made from crude boards. These contained the bodies of Stus and fellow Ukrainian *zeks*, Yuri Lytvyn and Oleksa Tykhy. A short liturgy for the dead was sung and then a vehicle bearing the packs set off for the city.

The next day, November 19, the funeral cortege moved through the city, past St. Sophia Cathedral and down St. Volodomyr Street, past the gloomy structures of the old KGB headquarters. Mourners led with a cross bearing a crown of thorns while the rest followed, singing one of the great hymns of the Ukrainian

Orthodox liturgy: "Holy God, Holy Almighty, Holy Eternal, Have Mercy Upon Us."

At the cemetery a group of former political prisoners took the coffins into their arms and bore them to the graves. And then, because no one but convoy guards had been present at the first burial in the camp cemetery in Perm, thousands now filed past the open graves, each with a handful of earth to cover the dead.

I think that's the widow among them, the woman in the smart black hat. She has a large, well-shaped nose and a sad, down-turned mouth. With a shapely hand she brushes her tears away. She is wan and middle-aged.

Mykhailyna is there. She stands at the grave and says farewell. I can't make out her words. I watch her on the video-tape, the solemn and inconsolable friend, and soundlessly make her prayer for her.

## — Last Will and Testament —

*Leap over the precipice*
*before you grow old,*
*and you'll fall into your childhood:*
*face up — into the scented grass.*

—Vasyl Stus

On April 25, 1979, Stus wrote a letter to his son. In it he remembers his childhood in a village south of Kyiv. He remembers hanging in his cradle from a hook in the beam of the cottage ceiling. He remembers the brown cape he wore to school and the dead bunnies whose tiny corpses in the dirt made him weep.

He remembers the childhood with the wheelbarrow, trundling potatoes from the field, grass for the goat, coal from the slagheap. He remembers the dish of food he tried to share with his hungry mother. He remembers her one torn blouse, her patched skirt.

He remembers he was hungry, and gleaning handfuls of grain from a stubblefield in his baba's village when a mounted guard snatched his bag and ran him off.

He remembers the first maps he saw—of ancient Egypt and Greece. And the first time he read Jack London's *Martin Eden* and Nikolai Ostrovsky's *How the Steel Was Forged*, and that he promised to study very hard and be like their heroes so that people would live better. He remembers a song: "Throw off my chains, set me free,/I will teach you to love liberty."

"Remember, my son, that people must live like the angels, with love for one another, with feeling; that all people are equal and honourable, all-powerful, whole, crystalline, made in the image of God. . . . For everything is alive and wants to live."

## — Photos from the Republic of Happiness —

Photograph of a street in Kyiv. Three men, two now dead. Summer (they are in shirtsleeves). The man in the middle, Stus, is talking, pointing a finger. He has a sweater thrown over his left shoulder. He is broad-shouldered, slim-hipped. His right hand holds a briefcase. It must be heavy: I can see the corded muscles of his arm running up under the sleeve. He is thirty years old and belongs to that legendary generation, the Sixties People, for whom the heady atmosphere of the early 1960s has already thickened and clogged with worry and fear as friends are plucked out one by one and vanish.

They were made prisoners at the first peak of their creative lives. They had been writing poems, painting pictures, developing theories. Then, they were working in stone quarries and weaving shopping bags.

But in 1968, 1969, Vasyl is still with us. He goes to the studios of his friends to see their paintings, he goes to football games, he lifts up his face to the September sun, crushing the withering leaves of the chestnut trees underfoot.

A photograph of Vasyl and some of his poet friends from student days. They are lined up on a couch, grinning, except for Vasyl whose head is bent down in contemplation of something on his lap. Thick dark hair tumbling onto his forehead. The sculptured cheeks and proud nose. The mouth slightly open. The shutter has just clicked. I have slid onto the couch beside him. I push my hand into his hair, groping along his skull, and pull his head back. He shuts his eyes. His mouth falls open and he utters a little cry. I do not let go.

He is surrounded by women. These are his friends, the ones who also write poems, who bustle about the one-room flat bearing platters of bread, sausage, radishes, torte, while everyone gets drunk and kisses each other in sheer admiration, who kick off their shoes and dance on the Crimean rugs, curling their arms around Vasya's hips and dragging him into the waltz, who shuffle off to the camps, too, and, thin and cold, their hair falling out and their breasts flattened and sapless, offer their blood for Vasyl.

Mykhailyna is here. She has written herself back into the festivities, the golden summers of their "small, temporary Republic of Happiness" where they found in each other's company relief from the everyday world of affliction and separateness. In their Republic they were neighbours again, confidants, audience, lovers, acolytes, at the core of which stood their poet, Vasyl. He lived as the "poetic heart" of their little sovereign republic, "like the good heart of a good king."

Where is the wife? No one mentions her. She is not there when, later, the surviving friends conjure up those celebratory feasts of their youth. Vasyl writes to her from the Zone, but the letters are so crabbed by the sour censorship that I cannot read anything there of his love, and I have found none of her letters to him.

And when I do come upon his love poems, none later than 1965, I am not relieved but excited by jealousy.

*tell me that you love me.*
*Just tell me about our love.*
*(Like the pulp near the cherry pit)*
*A single, solitary, round, damp*
*succulent . . . red word*

—Vasyl Stus

Jealous that, while I and all the other women dance attendance on him, offering our sighs and loyalty, he has cleaved to his wife and taken her to bed,

*so that gathered into yourself like a tiny fist,*
*you'll become whole and unharmed,*
*restored for my hoarse*
*gutteral whisper of joy.*

—Vasyl Stus

— MK —

A quiet summer evening on the Prypiat. The broad, gentle river rolling by. Motorboats puttering busily back and forth, carrying hay and some kind of fishing tackle. On the river bank, our small camp of noble savages on vacation. A few tents, a large wooden table, a firepit. Frying fish, a pot of dumplings, a bottle glinting in the pail of water. All of us were in splendid form, the men with paper bowties pasted to their naked chests. We raised the flag— lifejackets on a rope—and held our musical instruments—pots, spoons, plates—in readiness.

At exactly the designated time, the flag leaped to the top of the pole to the accompaniment of a great clanging and clattering.

From around the river bend came sailing a boat festooned in greenery. Two "nymphs" held aloft blossoming branches of plum while at the prow stood the tall, strong figure of a man whimsically draped in water lily plants, his head wreathed in wild grasses, and his hands gripping a stave. Poseidon! Magnificent, truly beautiful, this Neptune. Our friend, our poet, Vasyl.

And then he rounds a bend in the river and is gone. For awhile I hear the plash of the water disturbed by the oars and then that too is gone. The next view I have of him he is in the Zone, a hero among the damned.

He is thin, his hair is cropped, his camp uniform hangs on him like a potato sack. It's cold, the fire has gone out, the plank bed is hard and slicked with frost.

And then, in the final years, he becomes the dying man, his flesh melting away from him as he drifts off into a rapture of the spirit.

His place was where he found it — in his case, as it turned out, in a camp. Agreed, you say: all poets are citizens but it does not follow that all citizens are poets, and who will write the poems of the men and women weaving shopping bags in the Urals and digging gold in Siberia, flapping their arms and stomping their feet within the icy walls of the isolator cell? The task of the writer is to write, you say, not to sit (tongue-tied) in prison. The corollary is this: anyone can go to prison but only Stus can write Stus. Yet he didn't agree. Unperturbed by the epithets — spy, traitor, bourgeois nationalist — he got up from his writing desk and went to the Zone.

He did not hold on. I hold on. I insist on that broad back, the elegant line of the narrow hip in black trousers, the sinews under the hairy skin of his arm. I imagine the clenched musculature of his buttocks, the long shaft of his thighs, the dark, soft curl of his sex laid against his belly. He is lying on the grass. His bony fingers hold a plum, its blue skin split open, the flesh's golden liquor smearing his thumb. He shades his eyes against the sun. A small, pale butterfly lifts off from the cabbage plant and lights on his lip and he keeps her there, while she drags her soft powdery limbs into the corner of his mouth.

Remember how later, after the food and the drink, we went walking along the riverbank and talked and the air smelled of hay and mint?

# THE MASKED MAN
# IN WARSAW

*I*t's on Sundays, when Warsaw is hushed and the breeze through the half-open windows carries in the chimes of the church bells across the street, that I sense the presence of K's ghosts in the rooms of this small, compact apartment. Perhaps it is because I sleep in the living room, on a pull-out bed, that I am aware of them as they revisit the scene of their love. I know from K that, twenty-seven years ago, he was madly in love with the daughter of this flat's owner, but he was already married and she was too young for the lust to be consummated. I do wonder about this, though, as I feel little breezy gusts ruffling the surface of the sheets. K's story goes back even further, when he was still in short pants, and the flat's owner's aunt had been a family friend. Saying to his mother that she was taking the boy to the park, the friend instead took him with her to this apartment where she kept rendezvous with a married man. I wonder how K passed his time as the lovers embraced in this white, cube-like room. Perhaps he stood on the little balcony, half as tall again as the geraniums in the green pots, and whistled down at the passersby in a vain effort to mask the coital exclamations behind the closed pane of the balcony door.

I met K at a literary conference in Slovenia in May 1986 where, in the course of three days, we became besotted with each other.

He was not physically prepossessing. What attracted me was his public declaration in the conference hall in support of the heroic and persecuted Polish labour organization, Solidarity. Even three years after the lifting of Martial Law in Poland, which had been imposed against the embattled trade union, this was a rather daring act, especially on the part of a man who belonged to the Communist Party *nomenklatura* and who officially at least would have been expected to toe the "Party line" especially when abroad. That, at least, is how I thought of K.

I had travelled to Poland in 1984 precisely to meet unofficial intellectuals and writers, several of them in the Solidarity underground. I had had to memorize their names and addresses—nothing written down as I crossed borders—and telephone them from pay phones in noisy places like the train station. Some agreed to meet, others did not. It seemed to me that Poland was a place where it was unwise to speak too loudly, painful to breathe too deeply. And here was K, a bona fide Communist, a member of that elite restored to unchallenged authority on the bayonets of Martial Law, proclaiming in clear English, his name tag pinned to his good suit, that Solidarity had been shamefully repressed. I was aroused with admiration. We passed the three days in a near-frenzy of repressed erotic excitement, and then parted.

We corresponded for a year before we saw each other again. In his letters K revealed himself as a man of some complexity: the harried Party man, the unfaithful yet devoted husband, the lover of a desperately ill mistress, the literary figure, the traveller, the disillusioned political idealist.

For my part, it dawned on me that I had misrepresented K in my own imagination as a dissident. What I had really wanted was a lover from my own generation, one who had fought the student battles of 1968, the Solidarity battles of 1980–81, and who had then gone to jail. K belonged to an earlier generation who had joined the Party in its heady, reformist days of 1956 and then made endless little "adjustments" as the Party reneged on all its promises. Eventually I wondered if it were still possible to desire such a man.

I last saw K in 1988 and our correspondence petered out soon after. From time to time I would receive third-person reports of sightings of K as he adjusted to post-Communist realities, but this new democratized, market-driven Poland held no excitement for me and I lost interest in K as well. But the K of *Communist* Poland continues to haunt me, almost literally, since he and it are now historical phantoms.


## HOW I FOUND A POLISH LOVER

There was a Slovenian country picnic in the woods after the conference sessions were over. There was dancing. I danced with one partner after another. K was sitting over there, with the Soviet delegates and that excitable poet from Dagestan, and I rescued him—that's how I thought of it—by taking him by the hand and leading him to the dance.

He lit up with pleasure. He said he had not danced in fifteen years but he moved me smoothly around in an elegant little waltz. I was imagining, I laughed, that we were in a ballroom somewhere in the Austrian-Hungarian provinces, me in swirling skirts and he in tall black boots. He said I was some kind of angel sent down to make him dance.

Back at the hotel he invited me to take a coffee in the bar. We huddled over the little table whispering, although we were alone. Our conversation was keen, fluid. As we were preparing to leave, K asked me to do him the favour of allowing him to kiss my left eye.

After supper, he invited me to walk with him around the little lake, and so we promenaded arm in arm under the blooming canopy of trees. In spite of his stumbles with colloquial English, we understood each other perfectly. Our conversation, it seemed to me, was a kind of aria composed of harmonious parts of confession and interrogation.

His presence at this conference was a (guilt-laden) respite from the burdens of caring for the two women at the centre of his life: his wife stricken with glaucoma, his lover with cancer. I had the impression that his ministrations were conducted almost secretly, as though no one in the rest of his life in Warsaw must know he had these (sentimental?) obligations.

His voice was soft, his eyes heavy-lidded (they gave him what I thought of as a "rabbinical" look), his smile tentative. I felt that our tête-à-têtes were verging on the conspiratorial. In the 1950s, he whispered, he had been an ardent and idealist Communist, but now felt weighted down by two unpardonable errors of his own zealousness. Once he had refused to recommend a student bursary to a friend who was from the bourgeoisie. Another time, at a publishing house, he had turned down a manuscript, a memoir, that was very well-written but "steeped in religiosity." Again I had the impression I was privy to rare disclosures, and listened with suspended judgement. "Listen," I said to myself. "Just listen. You have never known a Communist from *there*."

By 1968, however, he was disillusioned but his wife, a Jew, convinced him not to leave Poland, even in the midst then of a vicious anti-Semitic campaign spurred on by the Party. "Poland is our country," he said she told him. "We both belong here. It is our duty to remain."

I listened for regret in his voice but heard rather the esteem in which he held this wife of thirty-two years with whom he was inextricably connected although not, I surmised, as a lover. He had lost his virginity with her, he told me, on a park bench in a snowfall. "It was horrible, horrible," he concluded, although I didn't know whether he meant the material conditions of postwar People's Poland (there were no private bedrooms, no back seats of cars) or the sad, frantic coupling of a boy and a girl reaching furtively for each other under cover of thin woollen coats.

We sat on our own park bench, our arms around each other. He said my profile reminded him of the origin of the Ukrainian nation in the excursions of the Viking princes into Rus. No, I said, I am a Byzantine princess. Or slave. He confessed it was exciting to him that I was a Ukrainian just as his wife's Jewishness excited him. Later I would think of her and me laid out together on a slab of Polish guilt, Polish lust.

A sudden, delirious love. Snatching kisses from K's mouth as we rode the hotel elevator to the third floor. But I would not invite him to my bed. He asked, in his courtly way, to be let in but I said that that sort of thing was far too easily done and I would not do it with him just yet. He accepted this, was even, I think, appreciative. My sleep was fitful. In the morning I decided, flushed with fever, that I would go someday soon to Warsaw.

*Warsaw May 15/86*

*He is stunned, he writes, about what has just happened to him, three of the most important days of his life, and he longs for it to go on and on, and it will, in his heart, forever. But he's not so sure of me, his dearest, perhaps I am laughing at him, at his imperfect English, but don't I understand how the secret language of love and tenderness is hidden within its lapses?*

*That last night together, was it not strange, our innocence? But this is how it should be done, these "Congress liaisons," excitement compressed into a few hours of Congress banality. How astonishing that he found a soul—so dear, so knowable—from the other side of the world.*

*And now that we have found each other, we want to know each other. He wants to know every inch of me. Ah that mad last night, tossing in our separate beds! The kisses and licks and sucks and strokes of a love he wants to make (I must forgive his impolite language), a love he wants to plunder from the inner, golden depths of my Byzantine eyes! Well, as I, his dearest, can see, he has gone crazy.*

Our "affair" continued by mail between Canada and Poland, the usual Soviet-era inefficiencies plaguing our communication with missed or misdirected letters, so that K very often feared that I had already changed my mind about continuing this "stupid relationship with an old man from across the ocean." Or was I ill? He would plead for news, then fill in the gap with lewd, enthusiastic imaginings of how he would make love to me when I finally came to Warsaw, out in the woods somewhere, on a blanket he even now kept folded for these purposes in the trunk of his car.

He sent me postcards: Venice, Berlin, Belgrade, Moscow. I mulled over his itineraries, how easily he moved east and west. He had to go to Moscow because he was one of *them*, but it was also true he loved Russian literature and went there as a patriot of Pushkin's verses.

He has been worldly so long he must know exactly how to order a cab, tip a sleeping car attendant, present flowers and kiss the fingers of neglected ladies from the west, order steak tartare and artfully stir into its bleeding interior the mucous puddle of a raw egg.

There may be people who hate him. The secretary who stands hours in queues for his train tickets, say, who hands them over wordlessly and then goes to stand at a bus stop in the sooty dusk. Once she saw a movie about a romance conducted in First Class on the Orient Express, martinis in the glass jug, the silk lampshade pendulating as the train rounded a bend towards Trieste, but now the bus rattles under her sore feet, and K packs his bags with shirts from London.

But always there was news of his two women, of how his wife must soon submit to surgery to save her eye, of how his lover, B, must undergo another series of radiation treatments— her pain was unspeakable, her courage undiminished—and K was trying to spend as much time with her as possible. His wife seemed to accept the situation. He was often beyond the reach of a telephone, but he invited me to call his home (his wife speaks English). But please, not to say anything to her about us.

I received his letters with mounting confusion. I wanted, of course, simply to admire K. Or at the very least to remain fascinated, aroused. But in the harried circumstances of his everyday life—in which all its various elements had to be kept rigidly separate, so that his colleagues at the magazine office, say, had no idea his mid-afternoon absences meant he was visiting the radiology clinic—I understood myself to be a distant though necessary correspondent.

*He wishes I would write more often. Isn't there a song about that, you know, just "drop me a line from time to time, oh my sunshine?" He loves me no matter what, even if it's totally unacceptable for a feminist to receive such love. He insists I should write.*

But I had wondered—what really would he do with yet another woman clamouring in Warsaw for his attention? I began to imagine long, solitary days looking for cafés, brief evening rendezvous in the hotel bar, the heel of wine, the shredded napkin, hands held under the table.

I was becoming afraid of Warsaw, of the mask upon mask my lover donned to make his way through his obligations. Which one would he be wearing when, on his arm, I would claim my room key from the hotel reception? Or would he already be in the elevator, hand in coat pocket, stroking his erection?

Why did this "affair" not excite me quite as much as it should have done? Why did another idea altogether excite me more, the idea of the *young* Pole, who had organized a strike of railway firemen, or the priest who had heard his confession near a pile of scrap metal in the switching yards?

It is Saturday morning in Warsaw. What is K doing? Going to the market with a string bag, picking out young lettuces and strawberries for his ailing wife who sits at home in a dark room, curtains drawn against the painful light?

Perhaps he meets someone he knows, they sit down in the square and drink coffee. He doesn't talk about me but he is thinking about me, especially when he is lying in bed awake next to his sleeping wife and he wonders if I'm thinking about him. He cannot quite believe that I want him and he aches for not having had me. Later in the day he'll work in his study, then perhaps listen to music with his wife (Schubert), each in his and her chair. Perhaps there is a small dog. A piece of torte on a porcelain plate, untouched. A painting on the wall behind his head, a portrait of the artist as a young nude woman. Serenity, routine, solicitude: K, *burgher* of Warsaw, in yet another mask.

A few months before my own trip to Warsaw, a friend from Toronto about to travel there himself telephoned me to ask for names of people he might visit. He had his own agenda which had nothing to do with mine but thought some literary contacts, especially outside the "Establishment," might prove useful. Several weeks later, having returned to Canada, he phoned to report. "Your friend K," he said, "is viewed as a tool of the regime by your other friends. He's not a garden variety Communist, you know: he's high-ranking." I professed to be interested but not scandalized by this information. I said I knew K was a complicated figure, even a controversial one, there were colleagues jealous of his professional success, envious of his canny survival instincts, and so on.

Yet, when I hung up on that conversation, I felt a faint shudder of nausea. Analyzed later, it became a warning sign of my body's recoil from the idea of feeling excited by an *apparatchik*, a kind of queasy shame that I had let his touch arouse me when I should have been more alert. Alert, for example, to the K who, over dinner in Bled, leaned forward to say that Solidarity had gone "too far." There were others at the table, quite possibly his "minders" from Warsaw and it was to them, I understood, the remark was directed. Still, he needn't have said anything at all about Solidarity. He might have commented on the food, the weather, his taste in jazz, anything at all but this gratuitous *correctness*. So even then, in the vortex of my excitement, I had felt the prick of contempt.

It was the young men in their prison cells, slender in the shadows, the ones who had gone much too far, who aroused me.

How would I go to Warsaw? Who would I be, as K squired me about possessively? In Poland, the question poses itself: is there a "private" in Poland? Is there a room somewhere where the derisory commentary of Solidarity would not he heard? I could keep my distance. But keeping one's distance is fatal to the erotic enterprise. There would be no possibility of delirium. And it was delirium that I counted on when I put my hand on his thigh in the bar in Bled and said I would come to Warsaw. Still, there is the erotic possibility of being debauched in the embrace of the lascivious comrade, the *frisson* of corruption.

Is there a narrative here, even if there isn't a love story? I begin to see myself at the Warsaw train station walking towards K, walking into his arms and, even as I lie with him for the first time, writing the text of my departure.

In wanting to write about K, his time and my romance of him, I am confronted immediately by a difficulty: so little of our conversation (as recorded in my notebooks) and correspondence actually was concerned with details of his life story. For all my curiosity about K, it seems I was either too weary at the end of visits with him to write out full accounts or, what is more likely, we were much more concerned by the here-and-now when we were together. And so I have had to construct a "probable" biography of K from less intimate sources, and then to embellish it with the fugitive dust of desire and receding memory.

## UNMASKING THE POLISH DISSIDENT

In Warsaw that spring of 1987, I knew immediately we would not be lovers. From where I stood in the baggage retrieval area of the airport I could see K behind the plywood and glass partition holding a cellophane-wrapped bouquet. Even from that distance he seemed shrunken, his blue corduroy suit ballooning around him, his body curved forward from the shoulders as though to fend off blows to his heart. Up close I saw that his hair and beard were greyer than a year ago and that the flesh of his face seemed to have slid off its underpinnings. I could see that he had no cheekbones. He was frail, not virile, distraught, not self-possessed, and even though he would bend over my hand to kiss it with a soft nibble of his lips and repeat that nothing of his feelings had changed, it was clear he was neither going to seduce me nor be seduced.

The present did not belong to us, it belonged to the dying B. K's caring spirit was saturated with B's dismal need. Her life force was dwindling, yet there was between her and K a *nuptial* faithfulness that I accepted. With K I had only the rapture of the past, on the shores of a Slovenian lake, or perhaps the rapture of the future in the Polish woods, a blanket, and a bottle of wine, miles away from B's grave.

Under the skies solid with whitish-grey cloud Warsaw lay sombre and featureless. This was Poland in the Spring of the Generals. Solidarity had vowed that, though the Generals would have the Winter (especially that first deadly December of the coup in 1981), they, Solidarity and the "people," would have the Spring. This was it, then: citizens stood forever at bus stops, hugging themselves against the chill wind.

K took me to lunch in the cellar of a summer palace of the Radziwills. After the meal we walked slowly, arm in arm, through the green sweep of the palace gardens and the cultivated stands of lindens along a small arm of the Vistula. There was a chilly breeze and we pulled our coats closer to our chests. "This is not my country anymore!" K blurted out of the blue. He described Poland as a nation of two hostile camps, the State and underground Solidarity, with himself as a sad, lone man walking a thin line between them.

I did not understand K's feelings about Solidarity. On the one hand he berated the movement for having "given up" without a fight. This was not, of course, strictly true; there had been resistance to Martial Law in the early 1980s, but the movement had then split into factions. Of course, he continued, it is in the Polish tradition to fight against all odds but even this hopeless romantic wreckage would be preferred to the mediocre politicking of mere survival. The politics of resistance, he seemed to suggest, had been recast as compromise, bickering, and self-justification.

I wanted to argue with him (as with myself, but didn't): who was he, in his safe sinecure at an officially-approved editorial office, to berate Solidarity for a lapse in revolutionary bravado? Whatever shabby deals the *real-politik* of Martial Law had forced the veterans in the shipyards to make with the authorities, nothing could diminish the importance of their courage in 1980 in leading almost the entirety of the Polish working class into strikes against (what one can only think of as) their history since the Second World War. Some had gone to jail, some were underground, others were in permanent exile, refused permission to re-enter their own country, many were dead. K would say he was "with" them, but had grown bitter and sad because Solidarity *was supposed to have made a difference*.

Just who was K "with"? At least one of Solidarity's advisers, he told me, as if divulging classified information, was a millionaire (from overseas royalties). The leaders all lusted after western television sets and refrigerators. They went to church. They were not Communists: what could one expect?

They circulated slander against K in one of their underground journals, claiming he had called for the exclusion of all pro-Solidarity writers from the Writers' Union. I looked closely at K to see how deep that particular barb had landed, but he was merely gloomy-eyed, and stroked my fingers clean of crumbs of the coffee cake with which he had treated me.

Unforgivably, Solidarity had accused his friend Z of being in the pay of the police as an informer. Z who had been chairman of the writers' association in Lwow (Lviv) at the time of the Soviet occupation in 1939, and who continued to show up at his office, right up to his arrest by the NKVD (Soviet secret police), keeping to his post while his fellow members had rushed off to join the Communist-sponsored union.

It was when he told me this kind of story, which he did not do often, and told it softly (with strain pulling at the crinkled skin around his eyes) as though he didn't even want an audience, that I remembered how I had fallen in with K in the first place. *Listening* to him, suspending all judgement, hoping for the miracle of fellow feeling.

Nevertheless I struggled to keep my erotic energy focused on K and away from the young men in denim, fists curled inside their pockets, grease slicking their boots, a gold crucifix at their throat, who sat in jails and swore revenge. Their buddies would remember this incarceration for them, as K had remembered for Z the many days of his lonely and absurd vigil in the vacant rooms of a deserted writers' association.

At another lunch in a restaurant in the former smithy of the Wilanow estate, we ate blini with smoked salmon and drank Bulgarian wine. "The situation is hopeless here," he said. "There can be no change. Technology and industry are crude and under-developed, we have nothing to sell, people are desperate to make ends meet. The Soviets will never loosen their grip and the Germans could come again." As for his own situation, he saw that, once there was no more taking care of his journal and his women, he would kill himself.

The trees were in full leaf near the Vistula but it seemed as though all of creation lay bleached beneath the sky. We shivered. I thought: If I want a Polish lover, I will have to dream him up.

*Who's Who In Poland* (1982 edition).

K., writer since 1949, contributor to a string of journals and papers, editor of prestigious quarterly, member of the Polish Writers' Union since 1967, of the Party since 1956. Laureate of the People's honours. Recreation: tourism. . . .

Decode: *Who's Who* was published in era of Martial Law but assembled in era of Solidarity, ergo believable. Long tenure at an official Party organ means K a reliable element, neutral in tone, invisible in stance, never taking sides in internal Party feuds. A survivor. (Example: his name not among those editors who resigned in 1957 in protest of direct Party interference in editorial affairs.) Doesn't mean he was a bad writer. Readers knew to start reading the paper only from page three, two pages after the verbatim speeches of the Comrade Secretary.

Note early territorial stake-out in the literary world, above the Party fray. As critic specializing in modern European literature, K has removed himself from the grubby arena of Polish literary politics in which writers, fallen into disfavour, drag their champions down with them. K's heroes live abroad.

The medals: so much blah blah.

Recreation: tourism? As far as I knew, K had never taken a trip without an invitation. He wasn't a tourist, he was a *delegate*. Did he imagine, though, that he had been his own man after all the toasts to Peace and Brotherhood had been drunk? That, in enacting without misstep these official deputations, he deflected censorial heat from his beloved journal? Or was he merely letting his bosses know that he could be trusted—give him a passport and he would go to the beach?

From Warsaw he had let me know his little book about Albert Camus had been sold out. "What a success!" I was happy for him. And pleased for myself that I could now speak of him as a man who had written a book about Albert Camus.

# — Ketman —

In Czeslaw Milosz's Cold War classic, *The Captive Mind*, a taxonomy of intellectual types in post-war Poland, I look for a man like K and find *ketman*. *Ketman* is the quality of a Muslim who, while in possession of the truth, nevertheless remains silent about what he knows when in the presence of his enemies and, in extreme situations, dissembles and denies everything, confounding the infidel by deceit.

In Stalinist Poland there were two kinds of *ketman*, aesthetic and professional, in both of which I catch a whiff of K's procedures. Torn between the compulsions of his own educated tastes and the obligation to admire the outcomes of socialist realism, our hero writes flattering reviews of the current theatre, then goes home, to the only privacy allowed him in a pitilessly public life, to read Schiller and Sartre in their original languages.

If Aleksander Wat, the Dadaist who died in Paris in 1967, is right about Communism as a doctrine of "exteriorization," then K huddled in his privacy to gain respite for his preyed-upon soul, and there he sat, alone, where his pliancy had no witnesses, nor his delicacy any company.

*Ketman* gave me a rather different view of the packets that arrived wrapped in thick brown paper and secured with coarse twine that I received as tokens of our international literary solidarity. They were also tokens of K's self-esteem, exclamations from a Polish writing table that here was an honest man trapped in a community of scoundrels. The collection of essays on western literature, the monograph on Albert Camus were all printed on cheap paper in covers already torn and mashed at the corners from their vagabondage in the mails. K was not a simple functionary, indifferently good or bad; he was a reflective soul.

# — What He Had to Put Up With —

Nothing escaped the scrutiny of the Main Office for Control of Press, Publications and Public Performances (bearing the handy acronym GUKPPIW), neither business cards nor obituaries nor the most popular periodicals. In a single year the Office intervened more than ten thousand times, yanking "difficult" paragraphs from academic theses to factory bulletins.

All this was invisible to the public, as was the stricken conscience of the writer who, anticipating his editor's or censor's disapproval, cleansed his own impure thoughts before submitting his text. As was the confidential communication, when something indiscreet appeared in print, between Main Office and editors such as K.

I try to imagine K at one of these meetings, his soft voice muffled in the boss's cavernous office, his choice of words simultaneously distancing himself from and protecting an employee from the wrath of an Office he despised. In *The Black Book of Polish Censorship*, published in 1984, I read of an incident at K's journal when the censor pulled a book review because it referred to the "ruination of writers" in Stalinist Russia. The thing is the censor had probably never even heard of Mandelshtam. K's humiliation was masked from the readers who guessed only that the words they were allowed to read had survived some discreditable process. I begin to understand his glee in announcing to me he will publish an exiled Central European writer banned in his country.

I arranged to have lunch in Warsaw, that same spring of 1987, with R, a journalist and writer who had spent twenty-five years abroad reporting from the Third World and who had returned to Poland in 1980 just in time for the Solidarity strikes and Martial Law. We were talking about his career, but I was listening between the lines for intelligence about K, for observations about Polish society that would help me understand his situation. And so R was describing pre-war Poland as a society in which people disagreed violently with each other's political opinions but would still associate socially. "Martial law has created a whole new situation: the impossibility of working with the state in an enthusiastic manner. Now it is of the essence who one writes for and who one socializes with." He did not use the word "collaborator" but I heard it anyway.

*Who one socializes with.* I knew it was creditable, if not honourable, to be seen lunching with R, even in a restaurant I was told was a Security Services listening post. He had lost his job as a result of Martial Law. But K? Friends pointed out the obvious: that anyone who could keep his status and privilege after 1981 was someone the regime trusted. This did not necessarily mean, however, that K "collaborated" with them. "The older you are," other friends interpolated, "the more you realize that this [Martial Law] is just another up-and-down."

Maybe. But when General Jaruzelski declared the State of War on December 13, 1981, the media and the journalists were the only two groups other than Solidarity itself to be attacked directly in the declaration. Most of the media were suspended and many journalists detained and interned. Before they could return to production and work, they had to appear before a "verification committee" and declare their support of Martial Law. Those who were not "verified" left the profession or moved to obscure journals. It eventually became a badge of honour to be blacklisted. By the same token those still with their (important) jobs were seen in some quarters as men and women with whom the army could make deals.

Yet it was not from K himself but from a colleague at his journal that I learned that, thanks to K's "understanding" with the authorities, none of his staff had to appear for verification: K vouched for all of them. It is possible that K, a gentleman and a scholar, sought to protect those in his charge from a scene of unforgivable vulgarity.

# — Out Among the Rumours —

I find myself in little scenes among Warsaw's chattering classes, sitting in small rooms on small hard chairs, breathing in the fumes of schnapps and Polish tobacco mixed with the dust shaken off the piles of curling papers in the corners of bookshelves behind my back. I am trying to be a good guest. I do not wait to be fussed over. I ask questions. I have brought flowers. I am also of course trying to put two and two together.

I meet M at supper, at the home of a visiting scholar from England. M is short, bearded and rather jolly, obviously in good spirits as he prepares for a move to North America where he has been invited to teach American literature. You can sense his relief, as though his relaxed body were already expanding to fit the comfortable dimensions of the American casual.

Now, here at supper, he can afford to be unhappy about his Polish university. It has suffered disproportionately from cutbacks because its rector has been "too tolerant of unofficial activities," for example of the unofficial student group selling underground literature right under the noses of the authorities. M seems unsympathetic with the students' situation. Because of them, he claims, the university has been forced to suspend its publication program and has budget enough only to send one professor to one international conference a year. M makes more money tutoring and translating in a week than he makes in a month's salary. "My salary is for cigarettes and one meal a month in a restaurant," he informs me with a wave of his cigarette, as if this were already a curiosity of Polish life with which he will entertain his hosts in America.

I am interested in M because a friend has told me "M has no use for K."

"No use at all," is the way she put it, adding that M these days "is close to Bujak." This would be Zbigniew Bujak, hero of the Solidarity underground, who has lived on the run, scattering a papér trail of theses, programs, and manifestos. I look more keenly at M, trying to discern the outlines of the intellectual in whom a hunted man would have confidence, but all I see is the jolliness.

Perhaps M is simply a professor with an active fantasy life about the underground. I pursue the story with two young anarchists: the story does not excite them in the least. "You hear all sorts of things," they say, pointing out that you cannot trust in rumours and gossip because you simply have no idea where their source is. Sometimes the source is the police themselves. The police will raid an illegal meeting and arrest all but one person — well, you can imagine the gossip that circulates about the hapless survivor! I accept this as an instruction to me — picking up stories at cocktail parties, for heaven's sake.

I think again about K and his susceptibility to gossip and rumours, and my own to his. Is this a surrogate life for the one lived by heroes in a web of conspiracy and danger, of which he and I are unworthy?

*I huddle under his arm in his car where we wait by the river for the winds to blow warm, and imagine myself under the blankets on the mattress in my lover's hide-out, a stone's throw from the Ursus factory where we met, knowing that it was just a matter of time before we realized our street was being watched, and he would wash the dishes, kiss my hands and throat, and slip away.*

In an extraordinary "roundtable" some years after the lifting of Martial Law former Solidarity activists reviewed their experience as anti-government militants. Their conversations were collected in a book, *Konspira*, which I picked up for a song on a sale table in Edmonton.

The guys (they are all guys) are remarkably unsentimental about themselves, but then everything had turned out all right in the end and they were spared the more normal outcome of Polish drama: martyrdom. It is shocking to learn that the historic Lenin Shipyard of Gdansk, motherlode of the movement and its strikes, was taken by two tanks. And that it had simply "never even occurred" to Zbigniew Bujak, so savvy and stalwart, that the army could impose a military dictatorship. Activists were "shouting and swaggering . . . shooting off at the mouth" while outside the shipyard gates the army was getting ready to shoot for real.

Underground, they learned that the crush of the public's expectations—Do something! Something spectacular!—cost several hundreds of thousands of zlotys for "actions" that lasted only a few hours, like the giant speaker installed in a cemetery that broadcast Solidarity propaganda briefly and then fell silent. Bujak described a tedious operation in which a group of people spent days and nights writing out information in tiny script on sheets of onionskin paper which they then rolled up into tight cylinders and hid in the washrooms of trains travelling west. Not a single cylinder, however, reached its addressee: no one at the other end had bothered to pick them up.

They could also be brilliant. At the peak of the nation-wide strikes in 1981 when telephone lines had been cut in strikers' towns, Solidarity "published" their most important news by scrawling messages on the sides of inter-city trains.

On reflection, Bujak was to call the underground a "myth of superficial heroism," a projection of the fear of losing face, perhaps, to the imperturbable General in sunglasses who had won. There were those who tried to put an "ethical" face on it. They refused, they said, to live in fear of a "piece of government paper," but even self-respect is a kind of performance. And the spiteful dream of outliving the colonels is pure braggadocio: "The Winter may belong to them but the Spring belongs to us!"

As they talk, another kind of self-understanding emerges: underground man as sexual lone ranger. One hundred and fifty-eight pages into *Konspira* here they are, talking about loneliness. Since partings are "burdensome," says one ex-activist, the trick is not to form any attachments, and to survey the women on the street not for their beauty but for the possibility that this one is a snoop for the Security Service, that one an underground courier. Beware the temptation to buy booze and pick up Solidarity groupies with the union's money just because you are "making sacrifices" for millions and they "owe" you.

Some did fall in love with a fellow conspirator and portioned out their loneliness or went into hiding at an old girlfriend's place—the wife's is under surveillance—where the woman's sacrifice of her own security and the respect, not to say awe, in which she held her heroic lover were a kind of company, the only "warmth" on offer.

You are told you are handsome, "more handsome than Belmondo," and brave and a beacon of moral authority . . . she is already taking off her clothes. Something shines in her eye that is not just lust. She generates her own heat. Take your pleasure and leave, before the first streetcar screeches on the rails below her sooty window. You are already starting to imagine the day you are free to go home, to dandle your babies, hug your wife, and watch television. Leave, while you are still the angel of insolence.

## A COMMUNIST CAREER

### — Rural Tourism —

*The children (beaten by the teachers) were given to lying, the parents were distilling 'moonshine,' the head of the regional council was building a house above the river with material stolen from a nearby official building site. Officials came to the forest to shoot—in the forester's lodge behind the village loud orgies took place. At night on the roads there were screams.*

As we drove around the countryside on afternoon excursions fleeing Warsaw (and B's sickbed? the fetid air trapped in the bedclothes?), K rhapsodized about the "German" villages of Pomerania.

Restored to the Slavs and Polish-speaking, the heart of Poland nevertheless was haunted by its German ghosts. My God, the pride K took in the bulky Gothic towers with their peephole slits and the ponderous brick walls of a church so massively planted on the Polish earth it seemed half-sunken there. And then there was the tidiness of the streets, the rectitude of the town plan, the efficiency of the railway, sewer system, post office—even People's Poland had not succeeded in disordering these.

We drove past the farms of the millionaire market gardeners who, from selling fruit and vegetables at exorbitant prices in the private markets, have built their greenhouses and their brick "villas" wrapped by verandas and arches. But this is only money. It is not culture, *breeding*. "We Poles have a nation but not a society," K claimed, one of those aphorisms I write down later and then wonder if he could possibly have said it quite that way. "Poles are uncivil, rude, and aggressive. They spit in the streets. They vandalize telephone booths. When they enter a building they do not turn the door's handle, they give it a vicious kick."

We pulled off the highway to have a stroll through Czerwinsk, not simply so that I could admire the monument: a huge granite boulder perched on a stone pediment that marks the place where the armies of King Jagiello crossed the Vistula in 1410 on their way to the Battle of Grunwald where they routed the Teutonic Order. And we stopped to look at the graceful and modest portals of a twelfth-century Romanesque church, but to have a look, too, at this "Dostoevskian village," whose caked and rutted streets, overhung with ramshackle wood and plaster structures, lead into garbagy courtyards. Crones and snotty children sat on doorstoops and wordlessly followed our progress past the bar, "Nad Wisla," where young men were howling drunk at noon.

Another time, on the way back into Warsaw from a drive through the Mazurian lakes district, we stopped for supper at a Swedish-built lakeside luxury hotel. All the tables were taken by the hotel guests (we saw their sleek and mammoth Mercedes Benz coaches glinting in the car park), and so we drove farther on into town. We found one restaurant open. K was downcast but also grimly satisfied that his disgust with "Polish" Poland was thus fully justified. "Of course there is only this one place open. It is after eight o'clock on a Sunday in Poland!" The kitchen offered one dish: boiled potatoes, a slab of pork trimmed with fat, and adhesive gravy. There was no beer or wine. We drank fizzy orange. There was no coffee. The tablecloth was soiled. The waiter was woebegone. I thought of the luxury hotel down the road, built by the Swedes; I thought of a plate of smoked salmon with a small crystal glass of vodka, and of Germans who come back to Poland to tip.

## — Germans and Their War —

K is a fragile vessel of memory. Compared to him, I am sturdy, stocky with innocence. I do not remember. I was not there. I sit beside him quietly in a restaurant, but he stands at a window looking north to the ghetto on fire.

It seemed we were always pressed for time and in the hundred topics for conversation that lay between us like a list there were only these three stories he offered about the war.

## — First Story —

Before the war, his father was a small manufacturer in direct competition with a Jew in the same business who in fact had won a contract with the Polish army. However, in the first months of the German occupation in 1939 their fortunes were reversed. Initially they both found themselves with factories they could not manage: the Pole's was trapped in the ghetto; the Jew's, larger and better equipped, was on the Aryan side. K's father effected an exchange on paper, even agreeing that once the war was over he would return the Jew's property, with interest. Instead, the man vanished in one of the deportations to the camps and K's father found himself briefly well-to-do, until the retreating Germans blew up Warsaw, and K's family escaped with a suitcase.

As I listen I am aware of feeling a kind of reprieve that it is K, not I, who has to come to terms with this story. *He was there.* We are both Slavs, virtually born guilty, we are always told, of Jew-hatred, but *he was there*. And I have no story.

Reliving his amazement, K tells me of Easter Week during the very days of the ghetto uprising in 1943. He was sent out, nine years old, with his father's money to buy French cognac, Spanish oranges and Swiss chocolates from suppliers in central Warsaw. Little K, basket over his arm, surveyed the bleeding roasts of pork, the amber liquors, the silver furs and the jars of black caviar while the Jews of Mila, Nalewki, and Swietojerska streets lobbed Molotov cocktails at the Germans and burned.

He remembered this cornucopia of European treats when he made his first visit West, in 1957, to Paris, and, standing outside a window display of a fashionable shop, was not so impressed. Perhaps he also remembered on another occasion how orphans chewed on shoe leather and delicately sipped water from puddles in the underground shelters.

One afternoon he drives me outside Warsaw to show me the remains of a *shtetl*. The single-story attached houses run in a row around the town square, all other structures destroyed. I am surprised by the normality of their appearance. I don't know what I was expecting but surely not these cottages with lace curtains, braided rugs on the doorstoop. K explains that Polish villagers had moved in as soon as their Jewish neighbours had been deported. "You can imagine how, well, displeased they were when some Jews showed up at the end of the war to reclaim their homes. They were supposed to be dead."

# — Second Story —

The ghetto uprising began April 19, 1943. A handful of young Jews, perhaps a thousand of them, in defence of sixty thousand old people and children hiding in basements from the terrible deportations, threw hand grenades at the Germans. This is not K's story. He was out shopping.

> *Qui n'a pas vu les ruines du Ghetto*
> *Ne connait pas le destin de son corps.*
>
> —Paul Eluard

It took the Germans three weeks to subdue them, the small arms smuggled in by the Polish Resistance having proved finally as useless as the Molotov cocktails. When it was over some respectable Poles came down to the smoking ruins with their children to view the last of the Jews being hunted down. You could say it was their cinema.

K was standing at the window of his parents' apartment, watching and smelling the dense brown-black smoke rising in a ghastly cloud above Muranow district where the Jews were being burned alive. It was so terrible, he told me, that when he first saw the photographs of the cloud that rose above Hiroshima in 1945, he did not gasp. Warsaw had exhausted his pity.

For years I remain impressed by this story and recount it frequently, this set of images of greasy clouds and cremations and spectators, until I run into a Pole at a dinner party in Edmonton who tells me—he is a film student—that the image is a complete cliché, used wherever possible, for example in the film *Warszawa Year 5703*.

The Germans rounded up the last of the Jews and deported them to Treblinka and then levelled the ghetto. The American journalist John Gunther strode over the rubble in 1949, noting that dandelions and cabbages had rerooted themselves in the debris of the synagogue. Eventually new workers' housing and parks were built in the area but, I was told, the rubble was never removed. That's why Muranow stands several inches higher than the city around it, steady on its foundation of bone, ash, and brick.

I try to identify with the Poles as the demon Slavs of Jewish memory, those Catholic villagers standing about in the perpetual gloom of their half-wrecked countryside, coarsened by hardship, who remember the beautiful Jewesses of their town and their fine clothes, and who were bystanders to their savage fate. Yet we also know that Reinhard Heydrich, *obergruppenführer* of the SS (in the film about the 1942 Wansee Conference to discuss the Final Solution), waved carelessly at a map of Poland and Ukraine and called them "the asshole of the world." Did he mean Jews? or Slavs? or both? He had called the meeting, he was the host, the power centre around whom the others danced attendance, and he had the last word, always. "We will not bestow better treatment on mongrels and other subhumans," he announced about the Slavs, "than on these eleven million [Jews]."

— Third Story —

In 1944 as the Red Army advanced from the east, together with the Polish Committee of National Liberation organized by Polish Communists, the men and women of the Resistance, the heroes of the sewers, were determined to throw the Germans off in an uprising of self-liberation before the Reds arrived. The order was given July 31. Against three armoured divisions plus tanks and machine gun nests on all the main buildings, the insurgents had some 2000 revolvers, 7-20 heavy machine guns (there are conflicting sources), 60-98 medium machine guns, 604 submachine guns, 1386 rifles, 25,000-50,000 hand grenades and 46,000 combatants with some 35 bullets per pistol. It was enough ammunition for two days. They fought for sixty-three days, in a city without water or medical aid. They ate horses, dogs, cats, and birds. They drank from puddles.

They had a postal service operated by Girl and Boy Scouts. None older than fifteen, these postmen wore the red-and-white armbands of the insurgents and slithered from collection point to collection point, emptying make-shift boxes twice a day, unless they were killed. Enter K's third story: as an eleven-year-old boy he too ran the gauntlet, emerging from the family's cellar at night, first to queue at the well with a bucket and then at dawn to run off to the cardboard boxes (his school satchel banging against his shoulder blades) and empty them. If addressed to a location within his district, he could deliver it the same day; across German lines it took two or three days. He was vague about whether it was he himself who crossed the lines, or others.

The insurgents capitulated on October 2. During the agony of the uprising, the Red Army had sat fixedly on the east bank of the Vistula, refusing to intervene in a struggle the Soviets counted on the Germans to win. They had determined that they, and the Communist cadres who peered out of their gun turrets, would be the "real" liberators of Warsaw, not those bands of Polish patriots going down in flames in the sewers. Every Polish Communist knows this story.

There were 300,000 dead. The Germans evacuated the survivors to villages and then blew up the city block by block, house by house, boasting that Poles would never again live there. They blew up libraries, schools, churches, gas lines, telephone cables, scientific equipment. They laid 98,000 land mines and then fled to Berlin.

After liberation, dignitaries of the Yugoslav Partisans, among them Milovan Djilas, whose memoirs I read, toured Warsaw and saw through the "charred cavities of doors and windows" the gutted chambers of houses "stretching endlessly, row upon row" out to the ramshackle shelters erected in potato fields, while the shabby men and women of the city shuffled through the rubble in silence, looking for something they could eat.

When the citizens of Warsaw were being herded out into the countryside by the retreating Germans, K's father left his considerable amount of cash and jewels in a suitcase on one of his properties. Along with everything else in the city, it was blown up. Thus K was able to begin life in People's Poland with a clean slate.

In trying to understand why the Poles of K's generation became Communists, I cobbled together stray observations from all my conversations with him that gave a clue. Bottomless class guilt for what his gentry-kin had done to peasants and Jews. Disgust with his family's pre-war values—their superiority complex, their vulgar jingoism -and with their Polish self-importance. In comparison with such useless emotion, K wanted to get something done. I remember his enthusiasm for the publication of cheap editions of literary classics "for the poor." After the war (K was thirteen) there was absolutely nothing to return to of the past.

Thanks to one of his father's former female employees, a socialist and later a Communist, he thinks he was spared the usual penalties of an accidental birth into the Polish bourgeoisie. K's father had treated her with consideration, even allowing her a day off from the factory to celebrate May Day. It was at her feet that the boy first heard the lore of the trade unions, of the bosses and the groaning workers, of the May Day fêtes of the super-exploited. And so when, after Liberation, this woman became a rather important Party activist in Warsaw, she "spoke up" for K and he was not molested by the envious and unforgiving. But I wonder about my notes—surely in *pre*-Communist Poland May Day was a clandestine celebration?

Curiously, he seems never to have been much of an activist. And now that it is much too late he is wistful about the life he might have had as a musician or mathematician, practitioners of the "pure." Yet, unlike many who were militants, he never quit the Party when the going got rough. Enlisted as an idealist, he did not retreat even as his ideals bit the dust in one tawdry regime after another. He would not break with his youth, the Party's "garden of earthly delights: miraculous metamorphoses, the spring of eternal youth," as Zbigniew Herbert, the venerable poet who preferred silence, recalled it, in an interview for *Partisan Review* in 1987.

It was on one of those excursions through the nearby countryside, which gave us now the only opportunity for an intimate moment —a hand on the other's knee, a secretive sidelong glance—that I mentioned to K that I had been reading the interview with Herbert and that what had struck me was the vehemence of Herbert's attack on the work of Jerzy Andrzejewski.

Andrzejewski actually meant something to me. As a university student in the 1960s I had had a whole education in foreign films, thanks to the long-haired cinephiles who organized a Film Society on campus and threw all their obsessions at us indiscriminately, from Kurosawa to Truffaut to Bergman to Ray. And Andrzej Wajda, leading director of the so-called "Polish film school." This was how I saw *Ashes and Diamonds*, Wajda's adaptation of a novel by Jerzy Andrzejewski, although I didn't know about the novel then. The film cast me into a black and white world, sooty, dreary, a first look into the world behind the Iron Curtain that was not crude anti-Communist propaganda. It was a world that seemed to me rather glamorous in a film *noir*ish way—good-looking men in black leather jackets caught in the lethal cross-fire of political principles.

Andrzejewski had been active in the literary resistance movement in occupied Warsaw during the War. When *Ashes and Diamonds* was published in the new People's Poland in 1948, it was a huge hit because of its sensational story of the Communist activist—as obdurate hero of the future struggling to be born—gunned down by the flamboyant scion of a bourgeois, ultranationalist, and reactionary family, representing "old Poland." He in turn is shot in the streets by the People's militia, dying a jazzy kind of death in the rubbishy alleyway—shadows, echoing footfalls, blood seeping into the muck. This at least is how I remember it.

"*Ashes and Diamonds* reprinted again and again, poisoning the minds of the young," Herbert fulminates in *Partisan Review*. "Let's not hide behind metaphysics. Let's not inflate ourselves like balloons. We are talking about primitive matters in a primitive language. But what does it really mean? The spirit of history does not exist. The system was built by people. One can list their names. First there was a small group of agents who attached themselves to the intellectuals, and the intellectuals played *Sonata Pathetique* for the new order. It was petty, foolish, pitiable, mendacious."

What does it mean? I asked K. Why this embittered tone? I wanted to know, for *Ashes and Diamonds* had not poisoned *my* mind. K's reply was long and impassioned as though there were a moral for himself in his preference for the ambiguous, flawed Andrzejewski over the pitiless, virtuous Herbert. If K was "with" Andrzejewski, then I wanted to be "with" him too, the conscience of a traumatized Poland struggling to be reborn as something good.

I took no notes at the time, but went hunting later. Andrzejewski had followed up his sensational success with a series of vulgar socialist realist works, including a travelogue of his official tour to the Soviet Union in the 1950s in which he sang the praises of the Soviet New Man. In K's estimation, he redeemed himself with his 1968 novel, *Apelacja* (published by an émigré press in Paris to avoid the censors). It was based on his observations about patients in the clinic where he was drying out.

His fellow sufferers were men and women cracking up under the pressure of their sudden elevation to Party posts. They were peasants marched out of their villages and enroled in Party schools to prepare for jobs in the police force or even elevated to the universities where it was not required they pass the exams. Then came the appointments that outstripped their self-confidence. Lost souls, they were drunks and failed suicides, and Andrzejewski restored them a kind of dignity by understanding them.

The party had its understanding of Andrzejewski too. In an interview published in London in 1987, former Warsaw Party Secretary Stefan Staszewski characterized the writer "bluntly" as a Catholic humanist intellectual who joined the Party of his own free will. And there, inside the Party, Andrzejewski wrote a novel, *Ashes and Diamonds*, whose function, says Staszewski with satisfaction was "to bring the nation round to this [Communist] regime."

The new regime changed everything, a Six Year Plan that literally electrified the villages and brought them the moving pictures. Still, the young people left in a great migration of the ragged-trousered into the new factories, barely educated, ragamuffin, shock troops of reconstruction. They were the proletarian darlings of the new order in whose name the Party nationalized practically everything, then bent them to their heroic task, rebuilding the war-blasted bridges, the flattened locomotives, and the mangled railway tracks. Herded them into foundries and told them to dream a city.

Between 1949–1955 the number of workers in state industry almost doubled. By the end of the 1950s they would still be dreaming of motorcars and television sets while drinking themselves to stupefaction with poisonous vodka in workers' canteens.

> *Un-human Poland, howling with boredom*
> *on December nights.*
>
> —Adam Wazyk

From among them, these distrustful, half-awakened dreamers of Eldorado, a few would be elevated to be their managers. Then they would crack up and be sent to lie morose and self-loathing in a sanatorium where the novelist Jerzy Andrzejewski would observe them through the alcoholic vapours circulating in his own brain.

K has psychoanalyzed Andrzejewski: a devout Catholic active in the resistance during the German occupation, he had witnessed such evil that his moral universe imploded, leaving him a sack of a man, twisting whichever way the wind blows. Guilt? Panic? Blankness? He railed against his fellow writers, denounced and humiliated them. Yet he found the reserves in 1968 to write a letter in solidarity with Czechoslovak writers now under Soviet occupation, and later in the 1970s to lend his signature to the protests of Polish dissidents. He never went to meetings but secluded himself in his apartment, sodden with vodka.

K, usually circumspect or caustic about his colleagues, seems almost filial in his defence of Andrzejewski who was old enough to have been his father. After K comes the generation of 1968 who see in Andrzejewski only falseness—the silence about the Poles buried in the Katyn forest or in Siberia, tortured, imprisoned, and worked to death. Perhaps K is "with" Andrzejewski simply in order not to be with his enemies.

My own earliest memory of a political event is the death of Stalin. It was March 1953 and I was kneeling on the mock Persian carpet with the *Edmonton Journal* spread open in front of me. STALIN DEAD, I read with satisfaction. I knew that Stalin was a very bad man and that it was a good thing that he was dead. I suppose it was also about this time that I was having nightmares of being chased down the back alley behind our house by men in long black coats. These were Russians.

Was this the moment when K and I began to desire each other? K was twenty years old. The great unravelling of Stalinism was about to begin.

They came tumbling out of the closets, then, the skeletons of the Communists betrayed and of those who had betrayed them.

From the secret cells in which they had been tortured to madness and death tumbled the skeletons of the fellow travellers eliminated as inconvenient competition for the hearts and minds of the workers.

Encouraged by Stalin's death, the Polish Party purged, dismissed, arrested, and extracted confessions. It was sensational.

In May 1955 K graduated from university. In another year he would be a Communist, but a *Polish* Communist, a socially-conscious Communist, a tender-hearted, well-read, and decent Communist.

In February 1956, at the Twentieth Congress of the Communist Party of the Soviet Union, First Secretary Nikita Khrushchev delivered a secret report to the delegates on the crimes of Stalin. Within weeks it was circulating in photostatted copies in Poland's flea markets. On April 20, 1956, 28,000 prisoners, among them several thousand imprisoned for political crimes, were amnestied. If the Party leadership thought it had by these tactics forestalled the worst of the people's judgement upon them they were foolishly misled. People's Poland was about to go on strike.

In June, the confrontation between workers and Party was so uncompromising that some eighty people died in a day and night of street fighting with the Security Police and the army, after which several army divisions set out for Poznan where they came under assault by grenade and machine gun and returned fire. Even the Party was upset.

At a Plenum of the Central Committee of the Polish United Workers Party in October 1956, after months of partisan struggle between pro-Moscow Stalinist old guard and a new guard in favour of "democratization of the relations between the masses and the leaders," the Committee made its decision. It elected as its new First Secretary a man who had once been imprisoned by the Stalinists, Wadyslaw Gomulka, whose name would become synonymous with a generation's hope before he too went down in the flames of the workers' wrath.

October 24, 1956, 400,000 people gathered in front of Warsaw's Palace of Culture in a crowd so dense that one man described how he was suspended several inches off the ground by the sheer press of the bodies all around him. They had come to hear Gomulka's first speech as a new-style Communist for a new Poland.

Party activist Janina Bauman stood near the front of the crowd and had a good look at the "little, grey-faced, withered man without any personal charm or wit," who the people of Warsaw nevertheless cheered and congratulated. *Sto lat! Sto lat!* He did not harangue them, he understood them, and he paid them the compliment of seeing them more heroically than they saw themselves.

Was K in this crowd? He must have been, he who was on the cusp of his commitment. We never talked about that day. But that K was once a black-haired, broad-shouldered Polish Youth Union member who stood unflagging in the multitude and heard the call to fortify himself with the revolutionary virtues of the working class—well, that's how I saw him.

I like to think that, had I known him back in 1956 I would have been moved by him, perhaps would have wanted to grow up to be like him: enthusiastic for the changes to be made, with my shirt sleeves rolled up, a shovel in one hand, a guitar in the other, and a red flag stuck in my back pocket. I might have stood with him at the gates of the car factories handing out copies of a cheap edition of the stories of Jack London or tagged along to a meeting at a comrade's flat, there to pass around duplications of writings that had just been confiscated the day before by the censor's office.

He had lived his first conscious years under German occupation, isolated within a Poland stripped of an unreturnable past, disgusted with the petty and chauvinist mentality of the "true Poles" who dabbled in Chopin, exploited peasants and congratulated themselves on holding back the savages from the east. Compared to that Poland, the Party would be "home."

*Bridge to the right*
*Bridge to the left*

Warsaw in 1956: there was no such thing as a taxi stand outside the train stations. Horses and carts still plied the appalling roads while 32,000 people lived in caves or cellars. The urban night-time darkness was almost absolute but the fired-up new steel works and car factories just on the outskirts of the cities lit up the shattered fields.

Something transformative was in the wind. At the American Embassy staff workers tossed books and records and United States Information Agency bulletins over the wall into the arms of gleeful Polish teenagers. Twenty thousand people gathered on the pier at Sopot for an international jazz festival and the crowning of Miss Polonia. In power, Gomulka cut the numbers of the security police, lifted press censorship and stopped jamming western radio stations. In response, Clubs of Catholic Intelligentsia formed and students at an architecture conference denounced "political professors" installed in the bad old Stalinist days. It was Red October, and to be young was very heaven.

Unlike the comrades in their thirties who had come of age during the Nazi occupation, those of '56 were in their twenties. They would have jazz. Aficionados of be-bop, they no longer huddled in secret jazz clubs to listen to the American Forces Network broadcast from Berlin. They would have jam sessions at the Dom Kulturny in Warsaw with the musicians of *Porgy and Bess* road show from the US and in Cracow impromptu concerts of street jazz in the streetcar depot where the police never bothered them. They would have new novels, western films, and new art at the Arsenal. Strippers would take their clothes off in dark night clubs to the rhythm of a poet's verses. They would have dance and fragments of *1984* and Ionesco. Of their Czech counterparts Milan Kundera would write: "They love their bodies. We neglected ours. They love to travel. We stayed put. They love adventure. We spend all our time at meetings."

Jan Tereszczenko, now an architect in Canada, in conversation with me about the period, remembered "the turning point had been the World Youth Festival for Peace in Warsaw in the Fall, 1955. For two weeks 15,000 kids from around the world confronted the population of what had been a sealed country. Hordes of strolling, crawling, fucking foreigners. I had Jordanian bellydancers in my house. A certain psychosis was broken. For the first time in my life since September 1939 I called my father in California. It had never entered our mind that we could dial the Operator and talk to California. That's how I knew the Iron Curtain was porous."

K was already writing for the official papers and would soon have the literary beat, so this must have been his world too. I imagine he had tickets to everything and a pretty good suit. Because he knew so many people he could reasonably be anywhere: the galleries of the avant-garde, the film premieres of the "Polish school," the new music festivals. Papers and magazines had become readable and so he must have subscribed to them all. And bought an East German radio to listen to the BBC, thanks to the rioters of Bydgoszcz who had smashed the jamming equipment. He joined the Polish Union of Writers and agreed with his comrades that émigré publications should definitely be allowed to circulate and bans on certain books in reading rooms and libraries must be lifted. Thanks to contacts in the Union, he was asked to review a book, later to do an interview on radio. As a Communist he met with comrades, genial in a small flat in Zolibor district over little plates of salt herring and pickles, mushrooms and sour rye bread, clinking glasses and arguing with passion —*because it matters*.

In Warsaw, almost thirty years later, I am looking at his body, his belly draped in a pale cotton shirt and buttocks lost within the loose-fitting trousers. I could pick him up and swing him around. His shoulders are squared off at the bone and curve forward as though to protect his sinking chest. He has small feet. To imagine him at twenty-three I puff him up, give him flesh and sinew, pull his jeans tight around his ass.

I give him energy because he must go dancing. I send him to the clubs and to the revues, Bim Bom from Gdansk, Wagabunda from Warsaw, then to the book kiosks to pick up Hemingway and Sartre, and to the All-Poland Exhibition of Arts at the Arsenal, and on and on, to the cafés when he droops, to the student wine cellars when he runs his tongue over his puckered lips. He has a different girl each evening on his arm, and she swishes her stockinged thighs under her swinging cotton skirt and runs her red nails up and down his tawny arm. He shivers. His thighs cut through the sticky night air as though he were a horse. Where's he going? He's a Communist and he wants to fuck.

On January 22 and 23, 1969, student agitator Adam Michnik (future dissident and political prisoner), almost a year after sustained student protests had shaken up Party and government, had his day in court. I imagine him still slender but with a sensual suggestion of fleshiness around his shoulders and thighs. Probably he doesn't bang the dock rail or glower melodramatically at his accusers. If anything he is a little pedantic. But he is ardent with heresies, and he recites them all for the court, from eleven-year-old red-neckerchiefed Communist scout to high school member of the Contradiction Seekers Club to twenty-three-year-old member of the university-based *komandosi,* who have seized the torch from the faltering Reds of October 1956.

"We believed," he addressed the court, "that the duty of a Communist is to combat every evil, every instance of lawlessness, every wrong and injustice he encounters in his country." In a nice turnaround he became judge, and acquited himself of all wrongdoing. After all, in that courtroom he was the only believer.

They say The Komando Kid, ex-jailbird, ex-Solidarity adviser, is now fat, and chummy with the retired general who once threw him in jail. But in 1986, on the cover of his book, *Letters From Prison*, the Kid is an angel. The shadows of the bars of his cell door criss-crossing his soft face fall around his brooding right eye and his plump lips like stigmata. Here, then, is the doomed lover from my own generation.

I did not mourn for him in his prison cell. It was precisely where he expected, even desired, to be in the wintertime of the generals' coup against Solidarity, just as he had calmly entered prison in 1968. There was no question either of his loneliness or sexual solitude. He was an outlaw. I might press against the bars from the other side, sliding the tips of my fingers across his mouth or blow kisses into the shadow where he slept, but for him there was no taking. The man who sat defiantly immured within the jail of the generals was not one to dream of creeping into a lover's bed to get away from the cold. Besides, he was an angel.

I have drifted far away from K here, to rejoin my own "Sixties" people. Born twenty years after K, the students of 1968 arrived with fresh outrage into political struggle while the men and women of Polish October had already made their "adjustments." The Kid viewed them with "affection" and "respect," but saw how they were folded back into the bureaucracies, orthodoxies and surveillance that had bred them. The Kid had wanted them to press on — "Show us the source of that evil" — but they had lost their nerve.

Another twenty years further on I meet K whose "October" was so ghostly it did not even cast a shadow as we danced.

There is a postscript to this, long after I have lost K. "A base for Polish democracy is being created today," Adam Michnik had written in his prison cell. "It lies in the moral sphere." More than a decade later, Poland has its democracy. Now a highly respected journalist and newspaper editor, a rare voice of intelligence in a sometimes poisonous political atmosphere, this inscribing angel is seen arriving at a costume party dressed wittily in the uniform of the KGB with "nymphets" on his arm.

I have a photograph from my last visit to Poland in 1988 taken in the courtyard of Warsaw University. My subject is a bulletin board behind glass. Something has caught my eye. Behind the glare of the pane and the smudge of the photocopier's ink is the black and white face of Che Guevara—waves of dark hair flying from under his beret, black parenthetical moustache over his lip. *CHE SI* has been stamped over his eyes so his expression is inscrutable but we all know that what he is looking at is the shining path that leads to the heaven on earth of *campesino* freedom.

I wonder if the Polish students see that too, or whether they see the soldiers waiting in the gloom of the little church's portico in the Bolivian village near Santa Cruz who will come out to kill him. Well, maybe Che sees them too, on the path. They will make him an angel.

## GENEALOGIES

*Dec 31/86*

*He writes me, his dearest, of this hardest period of his life. B has now reached the point where her bones are so weak that they splinter if she tries to move, cannot tolerate any more radiation. He has somehow secured a new, American medicine but even so, even in the event of a miracle cure, B will remain crippled. The fact is she is dying and he must stay with her, never leaving her alone for more than a couple of hours, it is the least she deserves, she is so brave and bright, and she deserves it from him.*

It was a very warm day and K proposed an excursion to the village of Lyszkowice in the company of B and her friend Veronica whose mother was the object of the visit. So I was finally to meet my dying rival. It did not feel like that, though, the rivalry. K seemed completely unconcerned; if anything, he wanted me to admire B, as if it were the most natural thing in the world that I, who had come half a world to be with him, would want to be his lover's friend. B, who walked with great deliberation, resting on

K's arm, smiled at me with drugged sweetness and apologized for her English, as we propped her up within a stack of cushions in the front seat of the car. She still had plump pink cheeks, but her hair was grey and wispy and I knew that within the flesh of her round limbs her bones were decomposing.

A Belgian capitalist once owned a textile factory (now a sugar beet refinery) in Lyszkowice and built a brick apartment block for his workers that represented the very highest standard of housing for the aristocracy of labour: skilled workers. That was a hundred years ago. Remnants of that enlightened world still survive, including Veronica's mother, the widow of a factory foreman living in reduced circumstances, as we say. This means that, crouched in pain as she seemed to be, she was nevertheless mistress still of these two largish rooms, the kitchen and the living/ dining/bedroom. There was no running water, only white enamel pails beside the stove, nor indoor plumbing. Outside, the faint perfume of the scorched lilacs succumbed to the stink of a pile of garbage at the bottom of the garden. The malodorous outhouses, presumably also a hundred years old, were still in use.

We left the way we came, along the cement floors of a dim corridor (the light bulbs had been stolen) pitted with foot-sized holes filled up with sand. Veronica assured us the corridor had recently been renovated. But the workers, unhappy that they had not been given an extra portion of vodka for their troubles, took the building materials home and repaired the state-owned corridor with sand.

It being a fine day of lazy-making sunshine, K suggested we break our journey back to Warsaw with a visit to the Radziwill palace at Nieborow. The Radziwills, Lithuanian magnates since the fifteenth century who owned thousands of rural estates as well as castles and whole towns and private armies in eastern Poland, seem to have put up palaces the way the bourgeoisie put up hotels. Their white and gold palace at Nieborow is pretty enough. I went wandering through the porte-cochère into the gardens.

There on the unkempt pathways under the lindens dropping their desiccated leaves I was stunned to find, like so much decor, the ribbed and pitted stone figures of the female idol of the Ukrainian steppe known as *kamiana baba*, woman of stone. They had probably been looted from Cossack estates during the Polish-Cossack wars of the seventeenth century, but even in that century were already ancient. Dnipropetrovsk archaeologist Dmytro Yavornystsky reckoned they had been carved by the Scythians and Polovtsi, nomads in the fifth and sixth centuries BC. Why? I wondered, discerning in their eroded rotundity the capacious belly and gourd-shaped breasts of the fertility goddess. And there the nomads had left them, in the high undulating grass of the steppe, to be picked up more than two thousand years later by a Polish grandee looking for lawn furniture.

## — How To Make Love To a Ukrainian —

And he will show me some interesting places in the countryside, K had written, the "mansion" that was his family seat, a country house where he spent his childhood summers. He was excited by the thought that, in the history of his family, this would be the first visit of a "Ukrainian lady" of Byzantine provenance.

This was becoming a repeated theme — our ethnicities — as though, now that we had forsaken carnal knowledge of each other we would explore the intimacies of overlapping histories. I had always found K's Polishness piquant, not so much as an ethnic essence associated with generations of heroic Poles who had taken (hopelessly) to battlefields and barricades against tyrants usually but not always from the east. I knew that as a Ukrainian I was supposed to detest this Polishness, but of course K's compromised situation did not lend itself readily to such myth-making anyway. But behind him did stand the heroes.

As to what he found so glamorous in my Ukrainianness, I was uncertain. The Ukrainians had been bonded labour on the great Polish estates of Galicia. Perhaps this is why he insisted my provenance was not of that uncouth ancestry but of the Byzantine, as I had once playfully suggested: blue-blooded, exotic, out there on the far eastern borders of European culture. But I did not really feel blue-blooded. I felt closer to the Galician, wide-hipped, bawdy, sly. If K was to lust after the Ukrainian in me, it should be that wench, barefoot in his kitchen, heating up his bathwater, the steam slick on her face.

Our first stop was the summer home of his grandparents where K, a bookworm of a boy who enjoyed being spooked by the ogres in the nearby forest, spent many summers. But he could not remember how to get to the house, and so we stopped at the tavern in Sochocin. There, pressed against a windowsill, small glasses of vodka hoisted to the sun streaming through the cigarette smoke, we were given directions by a grizzled drunk who, now that he thought about it, remembered K's grandfather very well, the hunch-backed doctor who refused to take payment from his poorest patients. "My father was a populist, not a socialist," K explained later, as though he would suffer posthumously from the misrepresentation.

As we walked through the grounds of the old summer house and then around and around the wooden, high-peaked building, its walls partially scrubbed of brick-coloured paint, K could scarcely contain his delight. I had never seen him like this, somehow lightened, his limbs buoyed by the air around his body, as he pointed out the large rectangular window of the room that had been his under the roof.

We drove on to the manor house (this is how I thought of it) which passed out of the family in 1935. K's indebted uncle sold it to a Polish farmer from Belorus and went off to Warsaw to join his brother, K's father, in his business there. We drove slowly into the yard, parked, and set off on a stroll. I could see silhouetted figures in the doorways of the farmhouse but they did not move and K paid no mind.

The estate was in a despoiled condition, its ponds scummy, the apple orchard gone wild and gnarled, the yards filled obstructively with bits of rusted machinery. Suddenly from within the orchard the farmer and his son appeared, both of them roly-poly in cotton T-shirts, and shyly invited us to have tea in the house. The exterior of the "manor" was dilapidated; inside, a musty air, humming with house flies, settled on us like grease. Tea in cups was offered and the farmer's own fragrant honey. Flies hovered over a torte and a pail of milk set alongside on the table. We ate, we sipped. We were invited to admire the works of art executed by the farmer's son, portraits of Christ and the Madonna. They were not bad.

I did not understand half of what was being said around me. On the drive back to Warsaw I did not dare ask K what it had been like for him to sit in the ancestral salon, burdened with good manners, while chickens squawked at the open kitchen door and our host complained of the "gentlemen farmers" in the suburbs of Warsaw who dabbled in tomatoes and cucumbers and drove the prices down. K's demeanour and posture had been absolutely correct, halfway between familiarity and stand-offishness, but perhaps he was actually mortified. After all, although for me the "estate" had proved just another farm, a working farm, for him I was a princess introduced to the aristocratic ghosts of time past; and flies had walked across our teaspoons.

It is the fate of the oppressed to be muted, the better for the master to be heard. Wordless, head down, cap in hand, probably smirking under his moustache, the Ukrainian has stood for a whole repertoire of brutes that terrorize the Polish imagination: shifty Asiatic, godless Orthodox, witless yokel, treacherous bandit.

But as a Communist K understood that if anyone had the right to historic grievance it was surely the Ukrainians, the Galicians, who had lived daily with the violence that governs the relations of the master and the servants. Perhaps it was the very intimacy of our contact that now nonplussed the Poles. They are all lost to them now, those eastern Galician lands whose dust lay at the bottom of the Polish heart like a paleological seam in which the oldest and dearest things of life, now debris, have taken root: the raspberry bush, the cream jug, the maiden standing inside the branches of the blossoming cherry, her face tilted up for a kiss.

As long as Poland had included these Ukrainian lands, the Pole was able to construct an alter ego to his own burdensome modern self, the Galician "other" who brought in his crops while he read Beaudelaire. Is this why the post-war loss of Ukrainian territories was so traumatic? Why the Ukrainian bandit who assassinated the Polish postmaster was the first hint that an entire people would slip away into their own country, leaving the Pole alone in his own unbearable history?

K did not feel this way, and it disarmed me. It was as though we formed our own little Polish-Ukrainian Friendship Society, toasting each other as we clinked glasses while the rest of Warsaw carried on, hating the whole idea. He had warned me about bringing up the "Ukrainian question" in public. "Poles will not be sympathetic," he said. I already understood enough not to attempt to speak Ukrainian in the streets. "They will think you are speaking Russian," he explained, thus introducing briefly the notion of Slavic origins even less salubrious than the Ukrainian. K would say: "I know the Polish army did things to the Ukrainians as bad as anything the Nazis did," and I accepted this as a token of his esteem for me. "At best," he continued, "Poles will make the point that 'some of their best friends' are Ukrainians," who are now elevated by that friendship to status of honourary Poles. Like his friend Marta whose husband was of Ukrainian origin. She had invited me to tea in a very nice hotel lounge. "But my husband thinks of himself as a Pole." I understood her perfectly. A Ukrainian husband who is no longer a Ukrainian is not a social impediment. But I was feeling prickly about this. What did she think I was?

I regarded K with a tumult of feeling. K had spoken always in English. It was our only language in common fluency and it had never occurred to me that this linguistic situation was anything other than practical. But now as we spoke of these new things, of Polish*ness* and Ukrainian*ness*, abstractions that had now become personified in our separate stories, it seemed to me tantalizing that English made it possible for K and me to say things to each other impossible in our old languages. The landlord and the serf girl, for example, had been doomed to play their respective parts: in Polish, the rapist; in Ukrainian, the violated maiden. In this new language, however, we were freed into a new theatre altogether. He didn't want to tell me, he did want to tell me, he shouldn't, he wouldn't, he did: it was just terribly exciting to him that I was a Ukrainian.

I place the melancholic lord at the wattle fence. He has his horse by the bridle and watches me at the well for several minutes before he speaks up and asks for water. I bring him the whole bucket. He lifts it too quickly and the water slops over the brim and splashes the front of his white shirt, plastering the fine linen to the muscle of his breast. He laughs. He drinks in gulps. He laughs again and this time looks at me.

The sadness has not left his eye but there is real mirth in the lines around his mouth. Suddenly he leans over the fence and grasps a stem of white daisy, snaps it and presents it to me with solemn gallantry. I arrange it in my hair. He should leave now. I can already hear the song that Pavlo sings when he comes in off the fields. Now the landlord, the *pan,* hears it too. He steps forward, his hip pressed into the fence, and bends suddenly with his mouth to my ear. "I congratulate you, ma chère mademoiselle." His foreign words tickle and I giggle, he gives a rabbity nibble on my earlobe. "On your forthcoming marriage to my ploughman."

He steps back, once again the melancholic *pan*. He hoists himself onto the horse and looks down at me. My hand rests on the toe of his boot. "Be ready."

Pavlo and I will be churched and escorted by our celebrating friends to his parents' house where the bridal bed is laid out for my deflowering. But I won't bleed. I will already have been pricked and bled on the rough wool blanket the *pan* lays out in the stable. He unfolds it as though he had kept it for just this purpose and indeed my sisters have preceded me in this ritual. Our chapped hands and calloused feet and thickening waist will be for our husbands, as will be the womb stuffed with the brats they make on us every year and the flattened teats the babies pull on, chewing them up with their little milk teeth. But our svelte girlishness, flat bellies and skinny thighs, our high, hard breasts, our fearful giggles as the *pan* pulls us down and reaches inside our skirts to touch us *there*, our bewildered, tearful anguish as the *pan* pushes, pushes his thick, glossy purple knob against the spastic resistance of our thighs and breaks us open as if we were bitches, our stillness as our breath returns to us—all this is the *pan's*. He is the master and he has the right.

## — The Eternal Triangle: Part One —

Imagine a painting with two focal points of light. In the first a Polish gentleman, a *pan*, along with his slim-ankled bay mare, his red velvet riding coat, his golden braid looping his right shoulder, glow warmly in the spotlight as though on a stage whose backdrop, the villa, stands in a discreet subtextual shade. In the second, a fainter spotlight illumines a pastiche: a fur cap, a muscled arm, the white shirt of a young peasant, his round moon face with moustache. He looks directly out at us as though to say the picture were about him: his youth, his strength, his audacity, rather than a display of the *pan's* property, himself included. For the *pan*, this is a picture of bucolic plenitude and of European civilization extended eastward from the villa out over the fields as far as the thatch-roofed serf's cottage squatting in the gloom of Galicia. For the peasant, it is about the tension, even excitement, of knowing something his master does not know: the Cossacks are coming, from the east.

Not in this picture but behind the villa in the washhouse is the woman. She too knows what is about to happen. She stands flat-footed in bare feet, her overskirts tucked up under the broad sash that winds several times around her waist just under her fat, pink breasts. Her white thighs are as sleek and sturdy as gateposts. Her braids are loosening. She licks the sweat off her upper lip with her quick flat tongue.

She is scrubbing her master's bed linen. That morning she had hauled it off his bed while he shaved at the window, and the faint antiseptic aroma of his shaving soap mingled confusingly with the musk of his naked body seeping out from the sheets. He sleeps naked, she knows this, or at least he is almost always naked when she comes in to get the bed linen for the wash. While she yanks at the sheets and pulls at the pillows she can "see" him standing at the window, pouring out a basin of water from the pitcher she has filled at the well, his legs akimbo. Once she had peeked at him through her eyelashes, had seen the brown sac swaying between his thighs, bulging with his balls. He splashed at his groin, then rubbed himself dry and tossed the cloth at her as she stood with the linen piled in her arms. She was looking sideways, at the bedpost.

She is thinking of Pavlo in the fields, of his thirst on this hot day and the sweat caking the fine warm dust of the wheatfield to his neck and feet and forearms. The *pan* is pleased with Pavlo's labour, the way he musters the lumbering oxen, wields the whetted scythe, rebundles the loosening sheaves more careless hands have bound. But she knows what Pavlo is thinking: he wants to kill the *pan*.

Pavlo dreams of running away, far east of here, to the emptied lands of Rus scourged by the Mongols, to join the other runaways —the serfs, the defrocked priests, the army deserters, the town adventurers on the lam—known as the Zaporozhian Cossack Host. They live at the bend of the sweeping Dnipro inside a wooden palisade just beyond the reach of landlords, tax collectors, and recruiting officers. There they hold the line against the raiding Tatars and Turks who regularly loot, burn, and ravish Ukraine, then drive their living plunder in herds to the slave markets of Smyrna and Crete. To the west, in the lands the Cossacks have deserted, their kin still live within the thrall of the Poles but they, fugitives, squatters, brigands, mercenaries, and warriors, live in the "empty, wild East" known wistfully to the Poles as the "divinely protected zone of freedom" as though the Cossacks act out for them the drama they no longer dare: emancipation, far away from home.

And now the Cossacks are gathering all across the steppelands, arming themselves and their peasant recruits and followers, untethering their ponies fattened on wild grasses, and boasting of fleecing the Polish landlords of their soft, white, powdered skin.

She has heard this. She is mired in necessity and repetition and cannot create her own activity, but the Cossack can, and he does it for her. She has worked it out in some detail while bent over the washtub. The steam slicks her neck as her arms plunge in and out of the water, the damp bodice of her shirt clings around her puckered nipples and her buttocks sway rhythmically side to side with each lunge of her arms. She can "see" the *pan* at his window, watching her.

Soon she will hear the scrunch of his boots on the courtyard pavement, sniff the man smell of him as he approaches her, feel his heft as he positions himself behind her, his groin pressed against the bunched-up cloth of her skirts over her hips. He leans forward on her curved back, his mouth in her unravelling braid, his hands pulling at her shirt until he has freed her breasts that swing now above the palms of his hands. He pulls at her nipples as if he would milk her and she stands quietly, penned in the stall of his arms. His knee kicks at her thigh. "Wider," he whispers. He too is hot and wet and bent to his task. He groans and gasps and weeps. When he slides his finger into her mouth she sucks it as though to pull him down her throat.

She is condemned to repeat this coupling over and over; even her pleasure is part of the necessity that traps her. Her Cossack mate will live beyond the eastern horizon, out of earshot, planning the revolution. She has been left behind and it is the Polish master who woos.

*Warsaw, Sept 14/86*

*There he was, my lover, holding my last letter (from July 29). Good heavens, it takes weeks for a letter from Canada to reach Poland. Just how are two people bursting with things to say to each other supposed to stay close?*

*It makes him giddy, this courtship and seduction of a woman of another language. This is the first time in his life that he is trying intimate communication in a language not his own. A totally unique, absolutely fundamental experience, this trespass of his linguistic frontier, a heady kind of smashing limits.*

*And love? Would I think it an exaggeration to speak of love between us? Yet he, a man of some experience, worldly enough to know that love does not easily find us later in life, is delighted that love has come again, and so unexpectedly. To him, at least. He confesses that he has had several women in his life—some of them maybe even prettier than I. He has no need of further seductions, except perhaps precisely this one, at the hands of a feminist, an independent woman, in charge of herself. At the same time he is intensely curious to know how such a sovereign woman responds while making love—is she still all control and reason, or is she finally soft and tender and maybe even out of control?*

*At the closing end of his sexual and emotional life, there is this other country where he would like to travel. A country beyond all his frontiers, a country of unheard-of sexual sensibility of liberated lovers. Eros's victim, he wants to be taken there.*

But by this time my long unfulfilled desire was going stale and I became distracted, looking out for a more promising avatar of revolution. Subversively, I had dressed K up in the costume of the Polish master, hoping for arousal in the part I assigned myself: his subordinated handmaiden. But he was only a bureaucrat who needed to keep his job and whose spasmodic dreams of deliverance in the arms of a Byzantine princess from the west were only meant to get him through the night.

## EPILOGUE

In 1989 life was rough in Poland. My friend N, writing from Warsaw, complained of the never-ending shortages in the stores, the stoppage of hot water in her apartment for weeks, "and now no water in the bathroom at all—a pipe breakage." A few months later she wrote again to let me know that K had written the introduction to a new edition of a formerly banned novel (and so I guessed the political environment was slowly reshaping): "he was trying to be so careful and cautious in regard to the situation presented in the book and the situation in this part of the world," she wrote of his rhetorical stance. "Nothing was expressed that could be held against the author at a later date." As for the "situation" in Poland, she added that Lech Walesa, the Solidarity leader, was man of the hour and that "everyone is talking pluralism, democracy, and a new type of socialism."

The cancer had reached B's spine and she was now undergoing a third series of radiation. Distraught, K wrote me of his helplessness, that he still had somehow to take care of her in this horrible time. Even as he wrote to me of the "happiness" he sought from me, I could only think of her bed in the hospital where clamorous birds awoke her in the morning, reminding her that there were those in the world outside the window who were not dying.

Later, he would send me poems she had written in the hospital. She could no longer stand the sight of herself in the bathroom mirror, her skull showing through thinning grey hair, dim eyes set inside a ravaged face she refused to call her own.

He had translated the poems, and when I read them I felt suddenly that K had become an intermediary between me and B—wanting me to hear her, understand her—but it was too late. I was always only a bystander and now I felt like an eavesdropper. She had surely never written these poems for a stranger to read. I had never hoped or even wanted that my liaison with K would cast a line to his sinking love. She was on her own.

In March 1989 B died. She slipped into a morphine coma and then died quickly. K buried her in a new cemetery in the northern suburbs of Warsaw and then wrote to me that, while he had expected her imminent death, he had never accepted it, this sentence of death upon her. While she lived, he could still believe that somehow he had managed the gift of life—he of the childless unions—but he had failed her, and life.

I worried about him. His ceaseless uncomplaining nursing of B over the years of her decline had been the only thing, it seemed to me, that protected him from the brutal encounter with his own self-disgust he knew was waiting for him. *He* had kept his integrity by finding *everything*—idealism, Solidarity, faith, revolution, dialectical materialism, authority, terror, progress—a disappointment. But even he understood that the Minister of Culture was a man with whom one must, in the end, make deals. He had found his little space where he was a decent man, with his magazine and with B, and otherwise was an exhausted and lonely human being whose body was literally curving over the emptiness beneath his ribs.

*Sept 19/89*

*And how was I? Did I have plans to visit Poland this Fall? Was Poland still interesting to me? He would be absolutely delighted to see me in Warsaw. I was to think of B's apartment as my home away from home; after all, B had liked me, having understood, in the most correct manner, the nature of our relations.*

*Luckily, he had much work to do — to finish a new book, to manage the magazine, and to manage a new job — he was now the president of a newly privatized company, one of the biggest in the country, apparently. But in fact he did not long keep the position and by the end of 1989 he was the worst he'd been since Martial Law in 1981: his beloved magazine was running out of money and paper.*

Solidarity had won decisively in the elections that summer and the government that took power in September was the first since 1945 that was not Communist. I couldn't tell if K thought this a good or bad thing. Four months later he was tramping through western Europe, cap in hand at the Foundations and Institutes: the Communist-sponsored publishing company, which had kept his journal afloat, had been dissolved. The company that had his latest book did in fact publish it and then collapsed, leaving K without author's copies or reviews. His only happiness was at the magazine where, in spite of having to let half the staff go, he was still held in high regard, still trusted. His conscience was clear, knowing that he had not been any kind of "commissar" of the old establishment but had, all these years, defended the magazine. I must have replied rather churlishly — perhaps suggesting the collapse of Communism didn't altogether suit him — for his response demanded that I understand him.

*Sept 21/90*

*He was quite agitated by my query about his "attitude" towards the new social and political order. Naturally he was with and for it. Who would not be happy with the end of censorship and the self-liquidation of the Party? The reason he hadn't left it earlier was that it seemed to him some-*

*how cheap and vulgar to leave a sinking ship. But neither did any of the new political organisms attract him. He was as free as a bird!*

But he had another reason to feel easy in his skin these days: the Minister of Culture had confirmed his editorship of the magazine. So, he concluded, he had no *personal* reason to be against the new government but did have a number of principled disagreements with it. He hated the anti-abortion law, the introduction of religious practices in the schools, the surge of Polish jingoism in public life and the "sometimes improper" judgements against Communists who were not necessarily responsible themselves for the old order's idiocies.

Writing in this indignant tone, he sounded renewed as the K who was keeping some kind of faith with his younger, impassioned self. But for me this had already passed into nostalgia.

*So, he will write me a long letter soon on Polish-Ukrainian literary exchanges, and sends his kindest regards.*

This turned out to be his last letter. It seemed we had nothing more to say to each other, not even on the question of Polish-Ukrainian exchanges.

N, however, kept on writing. She had sightings of K, heard gossip, ran into him herself. In September 1990 she found him "not quite so sure of himself" and anxious to let her know that his magazine was still receiving funds from the government, proving in his view that the cordial relations he had had in the past with Communist authorities were not being held against him.

In an undated letter that followed, N added that "no one has a good word for K," but didn't elaborate. In January 1991 she revised her views after having met with K in his office. "He is obviously on top of things again. A Foundation will finance the magazine and publish popular literature to make money. K is now on good terms with someone at the Ministry of Culture. This will drive his enemies wild. He asks to be remembered to you."

But the trail was growing colder. N didn't mention him again for three years, then casually noted that K's magazine had a new editor. As for K himself, he had recently been heard on the radio.

At the end of 1995 in Edmonton I entertain Jan, a Pole many years in Canada. He arrives with three friends and a bottle of wine. To encourage conversation, I have laid out dishes of herring, *kielbasa*, olives, dill pickles, antipasto, liver sausage, camembert, feta, and rye bread. All of it and three more bottles of wine are consumed with remarkable thoroughness over the next two hours as Jan, in a booming voice and grandiloquent gestures, tells us stories of coming of age in Warsaw in the 1950s. I give him more to eat, more to drink. He is hugely entertaining. I tell him I know, or knew, another Warsovian of his vintage. I mention K's name.

It's a small world: Jan had gone to school with K. And what does he remember? "He was very proper, even delicate, and never played soccer. He was always excused from physical exercises. He was a religious fanatic, wore a religious medallion and went to church—the proverbial virgin—but shortly after entering high school he began to date the daughter of a newspaper editor and some years later at our class reunion he reappeared as a leading Communist! Frankly, he seemed one of those weaklings who went whichever way the wind blew."

"Or a survivor?" I challenged. But Jan has a theory about these sensitive males of his generation: they came from "weak families," by which he means fatherless families. "In our high school class of forty-eight, maybe five had fathers. The war got the rest. So after the war there were all those mothers and grandmothers and aunts who made every possible effort to preserve the males, the sons, into the next generation. To preserve them biologically. And that was K: preserved for the future by a bunch of adoring women."

I had become one of them. But I did not know then that I was preserving him not for the Polish future but for my own purposes.

Dear K, forgive me.

# LORD, HISTORY FALLS
# THROUGH THE CRACKS

### PART ONE

### — Road Map of the Vistula Delta —

*D*ear Heart: Wacek and Hanna bundle me into the back seat of their car and we clatter down the E16 to its junction with the T83, through stolid towns of scrubbed brick and shaved hedges. We are travelling to Gdansk (Danzig).

I try to follow your traces, my finger bouncing off the blue lines of the road map as we skirt the edges of potholes. Drewnica, Ostaszewa, Szymankowo, Oslonka. Where are those Frisian farms of yours? We are on our way to Elblag; could that be your Elbing?

"Look," says Wacek, "order and civilization," indicating the grim slate roofs, the heavy-bottomed Gothic chapels. He is not being ironic. He means: Germans built these towns. Prussians. Not slovenly Poles. Wacek is a Pole.

Disposing of vast, waterlogged estates on the Vistula delta, German Catholic and Lutheran landlords in the early 1500s invited Dutch Anabaptists, among them Mennonites, to come dike and dam their lands. The reclamation of wastelands: it was to become a Mennonite speciality. The Prussians had the cities, the pious Anabaptists the reclaimed swamps. By 1608 the bishop of Culm (Chelm?) complained that the whole delta was overrun (his word) by Mennonites. Unmolested at prayer and labour, they had grown prosperous and eventually aroused the envy of their neighbours. This too became a speciality. The Mennonites would move, and move again.

There were elders of your congregation in Danzig from 1607 to 1788. Then they migrated en masse for the steppes of southern Ukraine. They would call it Russia. We would call them Germans. Touché.

In Gdansk I write you a postcard while sitting at the varnished table of a small, smoky bar in a cobblestoned sidestreet I will never be able to find again. It is damp with the steam rising from the moist wool jackets of the men who sit at the wooden tables all around me with tankards of beer, their fat thighs pressed against each other on the benches. I write to tell you some of this and to let you know they are playing John Lennon on the sound system.

You will never forget this. Over the years you will tell me again and again that I was there, in Gdansk/Danzig, drinking in a Polish bar, humming "Give Peace a Chance." That I would always be there, tapping my foot, licking the mouth of the vodka bottle, waiting for you to keep our appointment to hug in the smoky damp, kisses fluttering around each other's mouth like dying moths while it rains in the old street. You moon about a bar on the Baltic Sea. I leave you there and go east.

## — The Sich, the Empress, the German, and the Potato —

On the island of Khortytsia in the bend of the lower Dnipro, the Imperial Official Dmytro Vyshnyvetsky caused a fortress (*sich*) to be built in 1553 and then invited the Cossacks—five thousand Christian males, self-governing and womanless, hunters and fishermen and warriors—to man it.

*Sich*: settlements of Ukrainian Cossacks on the banks and islands of the lower Dnipro River, formerly trade route of Goths and Vikings down the amber road from the Baltic Sea to the salt pans of the Black. And first line of Russian imperial defence against marauding Tatars from the Crimean peninsula. They settled beyond the rapids and so took the name of the Beyond-the-Rapids (*za-porohy*) Cossacks or *Zaporozhian*, scourge of Tatars, Turks, and Poles.

Dear Heart, I am telling you all this because your Danzig congregations would succeed the Brotherhood as incumbents on the fantastic black loam of the Ukrainian steppes. And because the blood that irrigated it in revolutionary times would eventually be yours.

Runaway serfs knew to take refuge among the Cossacks, beyond Muscovite law, as did the defeated ranks of the peasant and rebel Cossack army of Emelian Pugachev who had taken arms (axes, pitchforks, cudgels) against Catherine the Second herself. A Don Cossack deserter and wily, illiterate, charismatic, Pugachev assembled a ragtag army—Bashkirs, Yaik Cossacks, Ural foundry workers, Old Believers, peasants, Tatars—that came close to threatening Moscow itself.

But after a hard defeat at Tsaritsyn in August 1774, Pugachev was handed over to the Empress's men by his own Cossack troop hoping to save their own necks, brought like a wild bear to Moscow in an iron cage, tried secretly in the Kremlin and beheaded before an enormous crowd in 1775. Stories circulated for years that he was still alive and would come back to attempt once again the liberation of his desperate people from this German czarina whom you would call Great.

*Sich*: A "political monstrosity," in the estimation of the Empress Catherine, who proclaimed its destruction August 3, 1775, a mere six months after she had had Pugachev executed. "Henceforward the use of the words 'Zaporozhian Cossack' shall be considered by Us as an insult to Our Imperial Majesty."

And so Grigory Potemkin, hero of the Turkish wars and favourite of the queen's bedchamber, dispatched an army unit to the *sich* and demanded their surrender. Just like that.

One of Catherine's modern biographers has written that the three thousand Cossacks within the palisades "gave in without a blow"; were then "removed" and "resettled" (in the plain speech of the Mennonite historian GK Epp.) I can't believe it was so easily done, Cossacks so meekly mustered out from the legendary fort.

I have been carrying about for years a clipping from a Ukrainian newspaper, written in the last years of Soviet authority (1988). It brazenly tells the story of how the *Sich* was overcome by Russian stealth and treachery, and "liquidated" by czarist troops under the command of the iniquitous Potemkin who could not tolerate, neither for himself nor his mistress, this "center of liberty, of rebellious antifeudal sentiments and protests" that raised the hopes of serfs and slaves.

The Cossack rank-and-file fled into Turkey and Turkish-held Europe, but their officers were arrested and sent into penal servitude in Siberia. Their eighty-two year old commander-in-chief Petro Kalnyshevsky, once decorated with gold and diamonds for his services in the wars against the Turks, was conveyed "in state" (according to Catherine's biographer) to his prison in the Solovetsky monastery on the White Sea where he was to be immured for twenty-five years literally underground. The Soviet Ukrainian version has nothing to say about the "six cartloads of goods" that accompanied him but it does describe his release, disinterred at the age of 117, blind, claw-footed, and smelling richly of loam.

The *sich* was razed, ashes ploughed into its foundation (salt sown into the pastures? the horses unleashed and driven to the Caspian Sea?), bits of embroidered sheepskin caught on the thorns of the bushes on the river bank, and the whole territory proclaimed "empty."

And what was this all about, sweetheart, this wilful disbanding of one of the Russian Empire's most effective, if mercurial, military instruments on the borders with Islam, this crushing of the legendary brotherhood of horsemen who would, for the next two hundred years, represent for the nascent Ukrainian people their best historical moment? It was to clear the way for more tractable settlers, among them the Mennonites from the muggy delta of the Vistula.

To quote Vladimir Lenin on the subject, himself quoting from a Cossack lament:

> *Hey, you, Empress Kateryna,*
> *look what you have done.*
> *Boundless steppe and happy land*
> *to landlords you have flung!*

Fourteen years after the destruction of the *sich*, in 1789, the first Mennonites arrived on the Dnipro and the island of Khortytsia. They came as immigrants to a land they believed wild and empty, to build fences and plant potatoes, and they would stay long enough to become landlords.

But just beyond their settlements, where the laneways of shade trees gave way to the disorder of the steppe, the watchful traveller could see towards the horizon the billowing dust raised by carters, their squealing wagons and their bellowing beasts tramping the so-called Chumak Road.

We waited, dearest, for a sunny day. When it came Seryozha took me to the outskirts of Odessa where, from a sandy hillock of the shore of the Kuialnitsky Estuary, we could see, under the clear taut skin of the pools in the salt pans, the pattern of the wooden stakes driven into the pans a hundred years ago by the saltmakers at the origin of the Salt Route.

Trundling over the steppe, leading a team of oxen and wooden-wheeled cart, the old Cossack, as white and flaking as his cargo, bore the blocks of salt from the Black Sea to Kyiv. A road was set aside for him, the Chumak Road, to keep his louse-ridden and mangy animals away from the sleek, plump cows of the Mennonites.

*Chumakuvaty*: to be a waggoner on the steppe. Cossack of the Brotherhood of the *Sich*: a travelling salesman.

## — Mythocartography: Road Map of the Motherland —

Dear heart, I am clattering along the ruinous highways southeast of Kyiv. This was my idea—this cheerless itinerary through a cold and ramshackle countryside. And my wish: to see the old Cossack lands of Ukraine, to see the steppe, to see the phantom carpentry of the *sich*.

Seryozha packed me in the front seat, a straw basket of tomatoes, apples, onions, and bread on my lap, plastic canisters of petrol in the back seat, and we headed south on this gritty, sleety highway that I had expressly marked: Poltava, Dnipropetrovsk, Zaporizhe, Simferopol.

Where are they now, those Menno villages of Khortytsia, of the old home, the Altkolonie, the *heimat*? Your people moved in from the Baltic and built and named them all again: Neuendorf, Schonhorst, Rosental, Einlage, Steinbach, and Kronsweide.

Where are your names? Effaced and relettered. There are Ukrainian villages here now, and they hide no clues. Guardsplace, Tankville, Collective Farmford, First of Mayville, Red Startown. *Tankovye, Sovkhozkoye, Pervomaiskoye*. My God, the nomenclature of the commissariat. So you too have been utterly forgotten.

In the 1930s, the Soviet authority, dreaming of cheap hydroelectric power ("Communism = Bolshevism + electrification"), flooded the fertile settlements along the Dnipro to create the putrid seas that lie like bilge-water over the bones of your villages and mine.

Declaration of the historian Olena Apanovych, First Lady of the *Sich*: "Waves of the man-made sea go on to submerge former

Cossack lands and undermine the banks. The Island of Khortitsa has lost hundreds of hectares of ancient Cossack land over the past years. The local authorities over the years distributed historical territory to build holiday homes, enterprises, whatever you like. Concentrations of industrial enterprises on this land, and the tons of toxic discharges, exceed several times admissible norms."

Because no one would give us directions, Seryozha and I wandered a long time on Khortytsia. When we came upon the museum parking lot we decided we must be at the right spot, the site of the *sich*. I stood in the parking lot. Behind me: phalanxes of pylons, colossi bearing power cables the whole length of the island. Ahead of me: stone crosses, defaced and slumping into the soil, and the hydroelectric works flung across the now-irradiated river in the triumphalist bravado of the first Five Year Plan.

On a fine September day in 1919 the schoolteacher Dietrich Neufeld ferried across the river from his house to the island. He waded through deep sand to get to the pungent woods. There he was surprised to come across what my friend and I had missed, walls of an "ancient fortification," he surmised the *sich*. Thoughts of Cossacks agitated him—"ferocious rebels"—so he turned again to the "mysterious lure" of the woods, and there in the sylvan silence "felt at one with nature."

Your Menno arcadia, darling, and my Cossack stockade: past recollection in the motherland.

## — The Horrible Wilderness —

It is said that steppe wolves loped into the new villages and onto the thick thatch of the houses where they would peer straight down into the chimney at the *hausfrau* preparing the evening meal, their squinty-sloping yellow eyes holding upside-down the image of the knife in the breadloaf, the babe in the belly.

Within eight years (1797) sixteen Mennonite villages were established on the right bank of the Dnipro and two on the left. They named this complex the colony of Khortytsia. Perhaps at night they caught a thin whiff of smoke on the down-draught through the chimney that still bore the velvety ash of burned oak and the gamy stink of scorched leather.

This "savage" unbounded openness was in fact the Ukrainian chernozem, prodigiously fertile. When the Mennonites finally met the Ukrainians, they called them "unindustrious." I can just see them, those Ukrainians, barefooted and weather-beaten, standing sullen at the fence, while the German beat at the bloody clods of the earth on Khortytsia Island with a domestic hoe.

Why did you call this land a wilderness? Your poets were wrong. "This land had never been broken before us, before we came, wild land," one of them sang. "We could grow anything, fruit and grain, watermelons. We planted forests."

That indomitable First Lady of the *Sich*, Olena Apanovych, twenty-three years expelled from the Institute of History in Kyiv, came back with a vengeance in 1990, measuring the volume of toxic discharges wafting over Khortytsia and lamenting the 49,000 oak trees on the island she says were growing in the mother-land when you arrived. She says you chopped down the lot.

## — A Typical Mennonite Farm in Khortitsa: A painting —

Sturdy brick outbuildings are nestled among plantations of deciduous trees, supervising the orderly gardens, themselves contained within white picket fences. Beyond the farms the wheat-fields stretch to the rolling horizon. It is a sunny scene of peace and fecundity. Who would not want to live here?

It is said that the traveller in the steppelands, wearied by the desolate plains and "squalid" peasant (Ukrainian) villages, experienced considerable uplift of his spirits at the approach to a Mennonite colony. For example, Baron August von Haxthausen in the Khortytsia District, 1843: "The fields are laid out and cultivated in the German manner; the farmlands and meadows are enclosed with German fences. Everything is German: the villages with all their individual farmsteads, the gardens and their arrangements, the plants, the vegetables and above all the potatoes."

And ten years after that, six million trees. Plantations, forest reserves, orchards, alley-ways. Oak, birch, beech, maple, elm, linden, acacia, and poplar. Apples, pears, plums, cherries, and apricots. Mulberry trees for the delectation of the caterpillar of the silk moth. Sheep! By 1825 the Mennonite farmers were taking their wool of imported Merinos to markets as far as Kharkiv, Poltava, and Simferopol. Some Mennonites were even getting rich. Between 1812–1841 the value of the cattle insured at the Khortytsia colony rose from 480 roubles to 2250 roubles. They produced three times more grain per household than the Lutheran and Catholic colonists (nothing is said of Ukrainian Orthodox households but one can imagine) and began to import threshing machines.

By 1919, when the schoolteacher Neufeld was surveying the Dnipro valley from a sunny slope above Khortytsia, there were steam-driven flour mills, farm implement factories, a brickyard, banks, shops, schools, and hospitals. "All around is the great Russian plain where thousands of villages and towns lie dreamily under a high blue sky."

Who would not want to live here?

— Notebook —

Why you, Menno misfit for brother? I'm not family, not blood. The things I don't know. But guess at or imagine. Your boyhood bedroom, the bookshelf, two books among several: the German Bible, *Treasure Island*. Freshly waxed floors. Bleached bedsheets flapping on the line. You on a bicycle, sailing around the block, making up stories to continue *Treasure Island*. Hymns, shunnings, folklore of the German forests (or would that be of the Dutch — of Dutch marshes?), ballads of the great wanderings, from Frisia to Prussia to Zaporozhia to southern Manitoba. Plunked down on the flat, wide, open, hot, and brazen plain.

Adolescence in a Menno town during seasons of bumper crops, and the uncles sell automobiles. Your picture in the high school yearbook (brushcut? geeky?), horseshit on the bottom of your shoes, sweating palms on the dance floor, fat prick under the front pocket of your bluejeans, the hair growing like barley silk on your belly, the boozy vomitings, tobacco on the bottom lip. You lock yourself up and learn to rock 'n' roll alone, dancing like a plains banshee, wind and dustbowl banshee, bleach-boned buffalo skull banshee. But you won't sing in church. And the church abhors your dance. How can you have rock 'n' roll without the dance? You will have it in language, its rhythm, its sensuousness, its music, that goes "mouth to ear, body to body." It's the only thing you trust.

## — Nostalgia of the Steppe —

According to the poets, the vanished Nogai (Tatars), horsemen of the steppes, made the Mennonites feel like intruders even generations after they were gone, when the farmer would cut open their burial mounds and scoop up their funerary articles, to make room for watermelons and potatoes. He felt keenly that his "German" orderliness of garden and prayer had been established at the price of . . . what? a mystery, an otherness. And, because the Slavs were likewise prior to the Germans in this place, perhaps their spirits haunted you too.

Throughout Arnold Dyck's *Lost in the Steppe*, the Mennonite boy Hans struggles with an inchoate yearning for something the "Russians" have and he doesn't, a way of inhabiting this magnificent prairie they both love: they sing, and he doesn't. They sing with sorrow, with fierceness, with foreboding, and they fill up his emptiness. Compared to them, he has only just arrived, interloper on the steppe, and he strains to feel what they feel: the weight of "a century below the sky." The songs are their knowledge of a land where Hans feels lost, a tumbleweed, an alien.

So, when the time comes for the melancholic Ukrainian peasants to rise up against their masters and *take back the land*, the Mennonites will say they are lost.

## — The Curse —

You will wander, like the Jews, far from the source of your faith. Where you settle no one will understand what you say. You will draw yourselves together as though there were no home except where you find your own kind; your neighbours will be strangers. In solitude and labour and prayer you hold yourselves apart from the temptations of the easeful world, but you will always prosper.

Your lands will get bigger and your herds fatter and your desires more insistent. You will want to be rewarded for your learning in the school and then to do better than your neighbour in business. Your wife will be industrious but your daughters will be dreamy and your sons will take up arms. Your grandchildren will speak a foreign language, and stumble sinfully in German. It will be time to move on again.

*"One hundred fifty years in Russia. One hundred thirty years Friesens live in Gnadenfeld, build this farm, and now just to get away we're runners and hiders. Na!"*

You write to say you have no homeland. It is the Mennonite

condition: "[O]ld history . . . strangers passing through the land . . . by choice devoid of nationality, of country . . . yet carrying the seeds of race wherever they went . . . their history an idea as much as a reality . . . a kind of separation of the self."

Yet somehow there is a memory of homeplaces, of the Frisian lowlands, the Baltic swamps, carried in the language your grandfather uses to tell you stories. "You go back far enough and you're from somewhere, I guess, but I'm not sure." But I guess stories are not a homeland. Still, I want to know: don't you remember being there?

The winter wind bears the prayer: Emigrate! *Aus wandern!* You feel you are only the step-children of the chernozem. So: two score folk pitching side to side in a cattle car north through Kharkov, north to Riga to the Baltic Sea. Men, women, and children with all their bags and pots and pans onto a ship that sails down the cold, grey coast right past the *alte heimat* of Danzig and clear down to Antwerp. Then over to London, over to Southhampton, over the Atlantic in steerage puking into the bilgewater. Off the ship in Quebec City, onto the train, and across half a continent to alight at Winnipeg and to travel thence, exhausted, to a precise squared-off piece of prairie meridian you will call home.

Are you mad? You had come to Russland precisely to fill the emptiness, to feel at home once again around barns and hayricks and the church, to put the ghastly yellow steppe to blooming, and you rode several generations in a row down the wagon tracks you cut yourselves through the sod on the way to town, a German-speaking town. You did all this, God's work, and then you *upped and left for Canada* and started it all over again.

It's funny: I have thought of you as salt of the earth, growing out of it like the infinitely renewing limbs of willow from which we weave our fences. But yours is a story of flight and the roots spread shallow: you have to be able to get up and go when you feel the pressure, the danger; you have to be able to shake off the dirt as though this earth were not beloved, and you get away.

Maybe that's what it means to be Ukrainian instead: to be ever-lastingly of this homeplace.

You left and we grew back. You are utterly gone. No one re-members you. You called my country *de Kaump*—you always were a plain-speaking folk—and then you took the Ukrainian name, *Khortytsia*, which means "greyhound bitch." I don't know why.

You taught us how to work for you, you taught us to plant potatoes, and then you left. Left, or were killed or forcibly reset-tled or hounded, hurled into box cars, and shoved across a bor-der. We had the folk songs and the name for the place.

I came back first.

This is for you.

## — Notebook —

I love this guy who kicks up his heels, kicks the can, kicks the traces in early Sixties Mennoville. I see him skinny and jerky and fair-enough-looking, his jeans too big for him and pulled close in folds around his waist with a braided belt. In white T-shirt and penny loafers and white socks, he's a boy strutting his stuff down Main Street, making up a story that he's Marlon Brando in *Wild Ones*. But his hair, his bones, his arms, his name are all wrong. He doesn't belong to the Americans. He belongs to the elders.

You grow up. You court and wed and bed. Let me think: the nights you made your babies. (I see you only in the dark. There is a struggle here. Something furry. Underground.) Mornings in full light at the stove, frying bacon. You tie your daughter's shoelaces. You piss in the blue toilet bowl. You sit at your "typer." The sated heart beating behind the poems about your son. (Son? Son? What do I know about this?) The alienated church. You refuse all witness. Stay at home and stare at yourself in mirrors. The lost Menno faith—"enemy territory" you call it in a letter—that has a topography all the same, the fallow presence of absence.

## — Dedication: "To My Dead and Living and Unborn Countrymen in Ukraine and Abroad, A Friendly Epistle" by T.H. Shevchenko, Poet —

*The prudent German plants his potatoes at the* Sich
*And you buy them and eat them with relish*
*And glorify Zaporozhia.*
*But with whose blood*
*Is this soil drenched?*
*What fertilizes the potato?*

The potato, dear heart, obsesses me. Have you noticed the way it keeps showing up in this story, *specified* among crops, to signify Germanness? Even Taras Shevchenko, national Ukrainian poet who grew up a serf, makes the link between the potato and that emblematic German virtue, prudence. Note that he scolds the Ukrainians who eat potatoes *as if they were just another vegetable.* Both he and the Germans (Mennonites) understand there is nothing casual in their cultivation: the potato may be a humble tuber but the German is planting it in a pretentious location: in the rich loam of Cossack disintegration and decomposition, the razed *sich*.

According to Vernadsky's *A Source Book for Russian History* and the 1842 Decree on potato planting, even when starving the peasants of the steppe would not plant the potato, let alone eat it. Yet Her Majesty's Senate as far back as 1765 had particularly recommended its cultivation. "Of all the American fruits and vegetables brought over to Europe none thrives so well in any climate and in respect to its great usefulness is so different from sown grain as this species of earth apples," the Senators opined. And published "for the information of the general public" methods of cultivation and uses of the aforesaid earth apples (*kartoplia* in Ukrainian, *kartoffel* in German).

However, once the Ukrainians got inside the households of

the Germans, they learned how to plant potatoes. They could see the sense of it: the potato was a sensible alternative to grain crops that could easily fail and cause famine. Through intensification of cultivation methods, the Mennonites were soon delivering surpluses of wheat, barley and potatoes to the Black Sea ports. Crucial to this enterprise was the availability of cheap labour, to wit: the Ukrainians.

So now, sweetheart, I have you where I want you: inside the Ukrainian story.

It's about land, of course, not potatoes. It's about the land that the Mennonites have and the Ukrainians covet but cannot afford. The Ukrainians, and other luckless poor, are landless and obliged to work for the landowners. There are many, perhaps most, Mennonites who think this is normal. Fortuitously, some twenty years before the Mennonites arrived, the Governing Senate in Petersburg had reminded Catherine's subjects that the "landlords' serfs and peasants . . . owe their landlords proper submission and absolute obedience in all matters, according to the laws that have been enacted since time immemorial by the autocratic forefathers of Her Imperial Majesty." As your poet says: *Peasants will never own farms.*

There is a scene in *Lost in the Steppe* in which a Mennonite father and sons, travelling by wagon to the nearest market town, are pursued at one point by a group of excited peasant children shouting after them: *"Dayte tvaybak, khozyain, kinyte tvaybak!"* "Give us a bun, boss, throw us a bun!" A footnote tells us that *tvaybak* is Low German for *zwieback*. I had always thought a zwieback was a kind of toast or crust, something hard and dry I associated with sardines and cheerless Scandinavians, but never mind, let it be a bun. We are told that the children in this little scene are not starving beggars but villagers hoping for a "rare delicacy."

I don't believe it. If these Ukrainian children are not starving, what is it about a "bun" that causes such pandemonium? If these children are not begging, then why does the Mennonite boy in the wagon toss out the zwieback to the crowd like a little prince scattering coins on his birthday? and why do the boys dive into the dust, wrestling furiously for the "bun" that has landed on the road, as though the one who gets it is the one who eats?

At the same time, a little boy running alongside the wagon stretches out his right hand appealingly. "Tvaybak! Tvaybak!" The author calls him an "urchin" and you can see why he would say that: the kid is using his left hand to hold up his oversize pants. Inevitably, he lets go of his pants to grab the *zwieback* and down they go.

It is the stuff of farce. We recognize it: the sudden, hilarious display of offended male dignity. We notice the piece of string or the frayed bit of rope holding up the clown's baggy pants and we know that, for want of a proper belt, the poor man's private parts are about to be exposed. *It comes with the territory.*

## — Education Levels of Ukrainian- and German-Speakers Over the Age of Ten in 1897: —

Among the Ukrainians of southern Ukraine twenty to twenty-eight percent of those over ten years of age were able to read. Among Germans it was eighty-five to ninety-two percent. The differences in male and female literacy between the two groups was even more dramatic. In Kherson province, for example, the difference between male and female literacy among the Germans is a mere 1.04%; among the Ukrainians, 26.35%. Furthermore: by 1889 most children educated in Mennonite schools were exposed to the Russian language, Russian literature, and official Russian patriotic sentiment through their teachers. Eventually they would speak Russian too, as well as Low and High German. They did not speak Ukrainian. Only Ukrainians spoke Ukrainian.

When you arrived we called you *nimota*. Literally: mute and dumb. Figuratively: dumb Germans.

# — Nomenclature —

You were never *of* us. You were of *them*, the Russians, the auto-crat, and his ministers and princes, who had brought you to this place of peace and prosperity, and you were grateful to them, and faithful. You would call this empire of Ukrainian pain your fatherland. Its language was Russian, and you would adopt it as you adopted these steppes.

But the German language gave you the names of things. It was what held you to the material world as you fled and settled. It would have maddened you to shed each time the names of things, as though God's creation existed in *versions*. This is what young Hans understands, in *Lost in the Steppe*, when he explores the world of his teacher's library in Hochfeld colony but finds the books unaffecting, alien, Ukrainian in fact. In them he does not feel "at home" as he does in the German books, even though the Ukrainian world lies literally on the other side of the schoolroom window. Sprawled in the field he hears the rising song of the lark. It is the same lark he has heard in the books he reads in German. Now he knows that, just as she sings in his dream-time and accompanies the German ploughman and shepherd of the land *over there*, so she sings for him here in the steppe. "It is a German singer, and sings German songs, in spite of the steppe. Does he even know what it is called in Russian? Oh, yes, 'zhavoronok,' an empty sound; no one should be allowed to call a lark that."

But we had our names for things just the same. We got here first.

# — Notebook —

You shaved your head and stopped drinking, and so I called you *zek*, gulag slang. You made me think of a bush rabbit skittering across an old pasture, dodging the gopher holes, slithering under the barbed wire. A barb catches a tuft of you anyway. You in your gulag of lost loves. You have no wife, you have wounds I could stick my hand in. Somebody else offers you the sponge with vinegar.

We sit in dark corners of cocktail lounges, me squeezed into my chair as if shoved there by the ghost of your ex-wife cheerfully making room for herself in our aching conversation. You've invited her, of course.

I don't want to know her, in all her Menno earthiness, now apparently disorderly. (This is your version. It will do.) I don't want the *story* of your love, all the scenes and denouements, the character changes, the plot twists. Then I'd have to imagine it, imagine *her*, wouldn't I? Put her into the scenes where I've got you to myself. Pry her fingers off your neck and intercept your kiss.

We stroke each other's fingers, earlobes, sweater cuffs. Our conversation is a decade long. I feel mainly a supplicant of your insight. Write it all down. Decode the poems for private references but they elude me. I make plans, arrangements, but you evade them. Fall in love with somebody else.

Zek darling, splayed poet under the lilac bush, banished husband, father at the sink.

## — We Want Land and We Want It Now —

On the hundredth anniversary of your settlement, the declaration of the village teacher, Peter Penner: "We swear before God, the Tsar and the Russian people to instruct our children in solid Christian ideals and love of Tsar and Fatherland."

Meanwhile, standing in an excited rage below the front porch were the Ukrainians. Illiterate and shoeless. Their villages were the property of absentee aliens, the Russian institutions as impenetrable as the congresses of the Eucharist. They were dragged with great violence into the world beyond their here-and-now by the impending drama of revolution and the promise of *their own land*. The land had been Mennonite 128 years when the revolution came. A blink of the eye: that's how long it had been Mennonite.

*Land*. You had it and we didn't. Eventually we would be given guns and slogans—"Peace, Land and Bread"—and we would march on your estates. But for now we merely kept our accounts. How do I know this? Your own writers tell me. You knew all along what was going on with us—the "glinting eyes" of Ukrainian servants taking in all your wealth: the mill, the stud-farm, the silver candelabra. "You in feather beds and three years just straw for me!" The proto-revolutionary grinding his teeth against the pain shooting from the welts on his back: a stablehand, whipped for insubordination. You saw that too, heard the grievance. "German landowners, fat pigs swimming in their own suet, demanding more and more while Russian workers slaved for them and made them richer." You knew we were stealing your horses right from the barns where we tended them during the day and were scooping up contraband sheaves of wheat we had stooked ourselves. "And then the arson last summer at Martens': wasn't that done by their own servant!" and then Klassen's belly slit open by a pitchfork wielded by the servant he had beaten black and blue.

In John Weier's *Steppe*, there is an uproar in Gruenthal village school when the teacher, Sergei Ilaryonovich Mechnikov (not in fact a Ukrainian surname), in spite of his respectable teaching certificate and status among the Mennonites, loses control of his national feelings. A boy has giggled behind his back; he strikes him across the side of his head. He is a geyser of indignation, as though he had waited generations for just such a moment, a roomful of shocked and weeping children who are being made to learn the lesson their arrogant elders have refused. There had never been a Ukrainian patriot in their midst before, only slacking, half-stupefied *muzhiks*: "You think we're drunk and thieves. . . . We're just dumb Ukrainians. You look down on us. You like to laugh, and beat us. Whose land is this? Do you know why we're so poor? . . . Whose land is this? Do you remember how you got it? . . . Someday you'll see the real Ukraine. You won't like it."

I think of those Westernizers and Populists and village school-teachers on whose shoulders the revolutionaries of 1917 stood, their dogged loyalty to a dream of *uplift* from the dark mud of the czarist villages sustaining them until the real event came along, peasants with pitchforks and their leaders with fire in their throats. And when the hired help and house servants showed up at your front porch potent with excitement, they "devoured" you with their "smouldering" eyes, and your daughters fainted. We wanted you.


## — Definition of a Model Farmer:<br>A Mennonite With a Compliant Work Force —

A trade-off: you will feed and pay me decently, you will show me how these Menno things are done (the sheep breeding, the cross-fertilization of pears, the carpentry), and I will work hard and without complaint. Otherwise, you can beat me. I will live in the barn and you will call me "blockhead" and I will try to pilfer what I can, but mainly I am here to watch you and see how these German things are done. One of these days you won't be here.

We live in your houses. We are your cooks, and serve you our *borshch* and *pyrohy*. We embroider your shirts and sing sad sewing songs. You get all sentimental about the dear Little Russian village. We lie with you, sometimes in love and sometimes in hate. Can you tell the difference?

## PART TWO

## — Whelping the Steppe Wolf —

Your mother's first words to me were, *Dai bozhe!* [Ukr. Your health!] Then: "So why did your people kill my people?"

It was Sunday at noon, after church, and there had been music—two young women singing beautiful harmony like Christian Country and Western—and an enthusiastic exhortation from the pastor not to selfishly withhold the "good news" of Christ from the world's benighted heathens. You were feeling a bit shaky but I wondered what there was to feel shaky about. The sermon had been so platitudinous, and now there would be food: potatoes boiled in their skins, farmer's sausage, coleslaw, chicken, Kool-Aid, cold plum soup, pronounced "mouse." I was feeling mellow.

Among Jews I would have been more or less prepared for the question, but among Mennonites? What on earth had we done to you? Because I did have some knowledge about the concurrence of Menno and Ukrainian history in southern Ukraine after the destruction of the Cossack *sich*, I wondered if the Ukrainian peasants, in league with Cossacks, had done something unspeakable to you too.

Your mother then denounced the anarchist, Nestor Makhno, and the slaughter of the 199 Mennonite farmers from God knows which and whose village. *Why have your people killed my people?*

To tell you the truth, I was never much interested in Nestor Makhno. I thought of him as one of those lost puppies of the Bolshevik revolution, one among all those Ukrainians, left, right and centre, with their hungry, bootless armies and their tattered flags. Nevertheless, I appreciated your intervention into the discussion. "Mother, some of our Mennonites ruthlessly exploited the Ukrainian peasants. Remember the story they tell of Makhno, that he had once been cruelly flogged by a Menno employer?"

I did not know, from reading Ukrainian history and literature, that Ukrainians were scullery maids and cowherds on Mennonite farms. I did not know they lived in the same provinces of Ukraine, let alone cheek by jowl. You were not in our stories, at least not as Mennos; perhaps you were there inside my grandfather's acidulous epithet, *prokliatyi nimets!* (damned German), reserved for one of his near neighbours.

I did not know about you from our narratives but from your own, the literature you wrote when you got to Canada and which I read as Canadian texts. And there, to my appalled fascination, I learned that you were my raging, guilt-ridden, trespassing boss or his loutish elder son or his bookish younger one. I learned about your secret-harbouring rooms and my orphan's homelessness, your plain-speaking God and my avenging revolutionary angel, Nestor. He blew in out of the prairie blue, scooped me up onto his wild Tatar steed, freed the cowherd, and lynched you on the spot.

— Notebook —

But you do not think that all stories must be told. It is the only way out of myth, you say—this leave-taking without story or significance. It is the only freedom. But I say, what about those who never did leave a trace, whom history never inscribed? For whom myth is not the untrustworthy grandiloquence of story, as you would have it, but the modest trace elements of people's secrets held in common? I look at your "freedom" from these secrets and see the sly get-away of a single man whose story is already accounted for anyway. After all, you belong to The Word.

## — The Ballad of Nestor Makhno —

This bandit, assassin, highway robber, pogromist, and scourge of the Mennonites was born Nestor Ivanovich Mikhnenko in 1889 in the rather important town of Huliai-Pole, smack in the middle of Mennonite country. His father, born a serf, died when the babe was ten months old, leaving his destitute widow to raise five sons: *And the boys? Work? Yes, they work. And spend. And sit all winter in the saloon by the market place. That is our lot, a woman's lot, drunken lazy men and a row of potatoes behind the house.*

But by age seven Nestor was toiling as a cowherd and getting a kind of schooling in the village until, at the age of twelve, he became a fulltime farm labourer. At fifteen he quit the land to become a foundry worker in town. In Al Reimer's fictionalized version, this is where he first finds strength in the company of his own people. When a general strike is called throughout the Russian empire, Makhno and the foundry workers gladly join it and its "angry crowds, ready for anything." Meanwhile, over at the factory owned by Menno burghers, no one was going out. The bosses had warned their workers that anyone joining the strike would lose his job, period. The *njemtsi* bastards.

We skip now to 1907 when Makhno was eighteen. According to a cryptic reference in the *Ukrainian Encyclopedia,* because of an "injustice" Nestor had "experienced," he now joined an anarcho-communist group in Huliai-Pole. Yet there is no mention of how such an unpromising youth would have made contact with what was in fact a terrorist organization. Presumably his raging hatred for the "German" exploiters spurred him on: in a 1947 version of his story, he "dreamed of the way he could some day 'get even with them' both for himself and others." By 1910 he had been twice arrested for violent activity, and the second time condemned to death but reprieved because of his youth. He was sentenced instead to a life term of hard labour in Butyrki prison in Moscow. He is said to have contracted tuberculosis there from long periods in solitary confinement and leg irons.

All accounts agree that it was in Butyrki that Makhno acquired the only real education he would ever have, general and political. With the help of the prison library and conversations with his prison mate, the anarchist-communist metal worker, Peter Andreevich Arshinov (who would, in 1923, become Makhno's first chronicler before disappearing in the purges of the 1930s), he studied Russian grammar and literature, math, and political economy. His intellectual and political hero was the veteran Russian anarchist, Peter Kropotkin, whose "selflessness and strength of heart and will" he had hoped to emulate in his own revolutionary struggle. Al Reimer's fictionalized account, *My Harp Is Turned To Mourning,* has Makhno poring excitedly over Kropotkin's and Bakunin's books hour after hour (with no explanation of how he got them inside prison) and projecting onto their annals of revolutionary conspiracy his own fanatical need for a day of reckoning: "Someday he'd be a political leader . . . . He would get out of this stinking pisshole somehow and go straight back to Gulai-Polye . . . . This time . . . he would be the boss. Nobody was going to kick around the pimply faced kid anymore."

Was he in fact so unprepossessing, the "shorty" and "monkey" and "runt" of the novelist's imaginings? In 1991 *Ukraina* magazine (when it was safe to drag Makhno out of the woodwork again) reprinted a 1906 photograph of the members of the Society of Poor Peasants. Makhno is seated, so it is difficult to tell if he is short, but he is not skinny. He's a well-built, good-looking seventeen-year old in a black shirt and knee-high boots, clean-shaven, with full lips and thick hair. He is much more attractive than in the famous photograph as a revolutionary, in a thick double-breasted jacket too long in the sleeve and too narrow across the chest, with a comically over-sized fur hat perched on his head, as though he were stuffed into the hand-me-downs from an orphanage. It is difficult to discern in this smooth adolescent flesh the man the Mennonites would call a wolf from the steppe.

Thanks to the March 1917 uprising in Russia which overthrew the czar, Makhno was freed from prison and returned forthwith to Huliai-Pole where the revolution was underway. His objectives for it were simple, if sweeping: all instruments of government to be destroyed; all political parties to be resisted, as they were all working for one form of new government or another that would defraud the workers and peasants of their liberation; all communal affairs to be settled by free discussion. He headed up the local Soviet of Workers' and Peasants' Deputies (elsewhere referred to as a Committee for the Defence of the Revolution) and organized poor peasants into bands that took an inventory of all lands and property in the region and proposed their redistribution. This sounds benign enough but belies the extreme social violence pent up in the process. As the anarcho-syndicalist Voline (who joined Makhno's army in 1919) would write of it: "During the time Makhno became, in his region, the soul of the peasants' movement, which was taking over the lands and goods of the gentry and even if necessary executing certain recalcitrant landlords, he made himself the mortal enemy of the rich."

For the Mennonite view of things, I refer once more to the hapless schoolteacher, Dietrich Neufeld, when he is visited by mounted anarchist troops demanding to be quartered. His nerves are at a breaking point; the girls of the house have flung their arms around him, crying for help. The "bandits" tear through the modest house, looting, but when they come across the piano they demand entertainment. The "spirited" Liese, with a "defiant glance," sits down to play a Bach air while the "wild, travel-stained brutes sprawled around in armchairs . . . [l]egs outstretched and arms folded like conquerors."

This is a leitmotif of Mennonite anxiety expressed again and again in the literature: this grave offense against property, especially domestic, intimate property, as though in a publicly communal culture here finally was the place a Mennonite could be violated: his living room armchairs.

# — Nestor Makhno, Author —

In response to insistent reader demand, *Ukraina* magazine in 1991 ran a seemingly interminable series of excerpts from Makhno's published memoir, *Huliai-Pole*, of which I kept one for my files. And now I pull it out, because I want to "hear" his voice separate from the clamour of those who spoke for him. It turns out to be the first instalment of the series and is introduced by the History graduate, Valerii Volkovynskyi. Although Ukraine is still a Soviet Socialist Republic at this time, it is in the throes of *perestroika*: the publication of the memoirs of this anarchist brigand reviled and then erased by the Communists is an important moment, the historian tells us, in the reconstruction of a national history. Other archival material related to the context of his activities was destroyed during the Soviet occupation of Lviv in 1939 and in an air raid over Potsdam in 1945.

Makhno always took a lively interest in what was written about him, articles and books, but was frequently disappointed. He was particularly irritated by the memoirs of N. Herasymenko, *'Father' Makhno: Recollections of a White Guardist*, published in 1923 in the émigré press and later in the Soviet Union. He charged that it contained only inventions and legends. In exile in Paris, he decided to write about his life himself, especially about that brief and meteoric revolutionary period known to history as the *makhnoshchyna*. Of the three volumes of his memoir, which stop with the account of events in December 1918, only one was published in his lifetime. His erstwhile comrade-in-arms, the pseudonymous Voline (born Victor Eichenbaum) edited, and embellished, the posthumous volumes, but "for all that the memoirs of Nestor Makhno are an original account of the struggle of the southern Ukrainian peasantry . . . to be rid of all regimes and powers and to fulfil an age-old dream: to gain freedom, to take full possession of the land and to become its fully empowered master."

I try my best to get through these few magazine pages. They are in fact translated into Ukrainian from Russian. Makhno could neither speak nor write Ukrainian with facility. He admits in his memoirs that he "mutilated" the Russian language in a most shameful manner. The British historian David Footman, in *Civil War in Russia*, calls the memoir an "illiterate manuscript" banged into a kind of shape by the faithful Voline. Later, when I read Voline's and others' accounts of the *makhnoshchyna*, with repeated observations about Makhno's verbal awkwardnesses and infelicities buried inside their chronicle of a furious social cataclysm, I will think of Nestor Makhno's revolution as a rage to find a language.

What I read, in this rather plodding text, is an account of some of Makhno's first days and weeks in Huliai-Pole. He makes interminable rounds of meetings, congresses and sessions, at factories and in barracks, addressing peasants, soldiers, and workers the sum total of whose political education consists of obsessive rereadings of Kropotkin and Bakunin. Already, in these budding days of the social revolution, he is worrying that it has "slipped into the noose of the State and is suffocating there, pale, parched and corpse-like." He sees his workers and peasants from the "humiliated village" in a struggle to the death with political parties and government for control of their own creation: free work, equality, and solidarity.

Then there is this moment: he is in the town archives, rummaging through police files, when he comes across documents that name those citizens who had informed on his anarchist group and how much they had been paid. One is a man named Onishchenko who he runs into later, in the centre of town:

"And now this piece of shit, who sold not only his soul but his own countrymen for police money, ran up to me, took off his cap and greeted me, 'Nestor Ivanovich! Good day to you!' and held out his hand. What utter revulsion the voice of this Judas stirred in me. Shaking, I shouted at him to get out of my sight if he didn't want a bullet in his head. Not even thinking, I put my hand in my pocket and nervously handled the revolver there, hesitating whether I should despatch this snake on the spot or to hold back. Reason won out over indignation and vengeance. Exhausted from these emotions, I made my way to the army storehouse and let myself down on the bench that sits near the door. . . . A free and just society, I thought, has nothing to do with traitors. They have to be destroyed either by suicide or by the hand of the advance guard of the revolution."

Within a matter of months he will have formed a revolutionary soviet to do agitprop among the peasants: *"All who have oppressed you, who have mocked your rights, who have grown sleek from your labour, shall die."* And in the summer of 1918, when Ukraine has been occupied by the armies of the Central Powers, he will command a revolutionary army and be known as *Batko* (Father).

For little over two years Makhno and his army (who at their peak numbered forty thousand men controlling one-third of Ukraine) kept their enemies at bay under conditions of appalling disorder, political treachery, and sickening bloodshed in the upheavals of the World War in Europe, the Bolshevik coup d'état in Russia, and the civil and national liberation wars in Ukraine. For two and a half years after 1918 at least eight different kinds of regime, with its army, ruled in Ukraine without any of them able to consolidate itself. Makhno was forced periodically to make alliances with one or another of them, especially the Bolsheviks who would then plot against him. That he also attempted to build and legislate—and did so, with interesting results—in whatever pacified social space he could occupy in and around Huliai-Pole is a bitter reminder that, as an anarchist, he had not meant to go to war but to stay at home and work.

For three or four months in late 1919 Makhno was not only a guerrilla leader but the head of what amounted to a free republic of peasants, workers, and insurgents. In towns he and his *makhnovtsi* controlled, notices went up informing residents that the place was, temporarily, occupied by the Revolutionary Insurgent Army, a force in the service of no government, no political party and no dictatorship. *"On the contrary it strives to protect the freedom of action, the free life of the workers, against all exploitation and domination. The liberty of the toilers is their own possession. The Army is willing to help and to advise but will not govern and will not give orders."* The peasants and workers proceeded to break up the estates, assume management of their little factories, arrange the direct exchange of grain for manufactured goods, and to name in an ecumenical spirit their very first commune after Rosa Luxemburg, a German communist.

Freedom of the press, expression, conscience, and assembly were guaranteed. Prisons were dynamited and demolished, accompanied by the enthusiastic cheers of the proletarian multitude. There was talk of opening schools to implement the pedagogical ideas of the Spanish Anarchist Francisco Ferrer but, with teachers having fled, it seems unlikely they had the chance to carry it out before war struck again. Voline tells us that theatrical performances were resumed, inspired by the new ideas, but does not elaborate.

For all Makhno's sterling quality as a steadfast libertarian and organizational and military genius, "I regret to say," writes Voline, "that the moral qualities of Makhno himself and of many of his friends and collaborators were not entirely equal to the strains that were imposed on them." He mentions debauched, drink-sodden "orgies" that were little better than gang rapes by men who had spent months marauding the countryside, "swift as the wind," seeking out estates to plunder and "bourgeois" to massacre. *"Death to all who remove from peasants and workers the fruits of their Revolution!"* Then they in turn would be chased out of towns and villages by the approaching army of an opponent. Because of a nightmarish typhus epidemic that felled troops and civilians alike amid the filth and confusion of the provincial capital, Ekaterinoslav, the *makhnovtsi* were forced to evacuate well before they could make any progress on the formation of free associations. They were out in the steppe, hauling on long trains of carts their wounded and dying.

In spite of an amicable 1919 tactical agreement for a military alliance between the Bolsheviks and the Makhnovites against the anti-Bolshevik forces of General Denikin, there was bad faith all around. In May 1919 there were active efforts to assassinate Makhno but he avoided the traps set in the cities.

In January 1920, refusing to give up, Commissar of War and Red Army commander Leon Trotsky was cabling Stalin, cool as a cucumber: "Do you think it would be possible to encircle Makhno right away and carry out a complete liquidation?" This, while Makhno was still officially an ally! If Trotsky couldn't lay his hands on the man himself, he would pursue the followers. In 1920 after a battle in the Crimea of combined Bolshevik and Makhnovite forces against Baron Wrangel's anti-Bolshevik Whites, Trotsky is said to have ordered the execution of the five thousand *makhnovtsi* who survived.

It was the beginning of the end. Over months of savage struggle for control of the Ukrainian south, towns and villages changed hands repeatedly. When the Reds moved in, they hanged the Makhnovite supporters; when it was the turn of the Makhnovites, they executed all the Bolshevik activists they could lay their hands on. The exhausted peasants eventually had no grain or horses to supply anybody and prayed only for peace. Both Voline and Arshinov calculate 200,000 peasants were killed by the Reds; there is no mention of the numbers who perished, one way or another, under Makhnovite administration. In the winter of 1920-21, Makhno, unable to hold Huliai-Pole against four Red Army corps, retreated north. Now and then he captured a small town, seized its printing press and ran off leaflets demanding free Soviets. But he was weakening, physically and materially, and he lost every one of his thirteen commanders. In August 1921, after three more skirmishes, Makhno was forced to flee with a handful of survivors across the Romanian border, leaving behind mere remnants of his army that were soon crushed. After three arrests, two escapes, and internment he finally settled in Paris. For the next fourteen years he eked out a miserable existence, spending much of his time sitting on a bench in the Bois de Vincennes.

He had a wife, Halyna Andreyevna Kusmenko, who stood a head taller and could handle a machine gun, and a daughter, Lucia—a *pater familias* in Paris, where he is already dying, home-sick village boy. It is told that he had a dream in Paris of being a simple peasant in Ukraine, married to a village girl, in possession of a carriage and fine horses. His enemies don't even bother to arrange his assassination; they just stop talking about him. He disappears.

In 1935 at the age of forty-six he was admitted in the last stages of tuberculosis to the paupers' hospital near Père Lachaise cemetery where he died. He was cremated and his ashes placed in an urn behind a plaque that bears simply his name.

— Ring of Fire —

*Makhno lies long dead,*
*festering in the wound;*
*his grave, beneath some*
*foreign soil, is a stigma.*

—Patrick Friesen,
"Nestor Makhno: Anarchist"

*Makhnoshchyna:* the hundred-mile-raids under the black flag of anarchism, as Makhno and his acolytes bring the good news to the exhausted villages of the transformation they are about to endure. All lands and factories are to be converted into social property: "You and you and you shall own them!" The state will disappear as a form of authority. *Makhnoshchyna* will be recorded in the Great Soviet Encyclopedia as a "criminal-anarchist counter-revolution."

"Swift as the wind, intrepid, pitiless towards their enemies," wrote Voline, "[the *Makhnovtsi*] fell thunderously upon some estate, massacred all the sworn enemies of the peasants and disappeared as rapidly as they had come." The next day they would be one hundred kilometres away and the day after that one hundred kilometres in the opposite direction before vanishing again from under the noses of the enemy militia.

Elsewhere Makhno jumps trains to avoid arrest, issues secret circulars from councils of war, or, badly wounded, insists on riding, with drawn sabre and cheers, straight into the machine guns of the enemy. Bullets go in one cheek and out the other, through the thigh and out the belly.

From John Reshetar Jr., historian of the Ukrainian revolution, we know that Makhno had a "burning desire to deliver orations." I imagine him lingering long enough to make a speech in the village green, surrounded by ragged peasants who had seen the last of their stores of grain hauled away by whichever marauding army had just beat a hasty retreat. *"Let the noblemen and landlords beware: all who have persecuted the peasants have been marked and condemned to death. They are vicious, well-armed and organized. We must be no less. So has come the hour of insurrection: Go and make it!"* And fantastically they did.

— Notebook —

That Nestor Makhno had an idea—an idea that you can find in European books—has never occurred to you. To you he was only a body that laboured and sweated and shat in the barn, raped when overtaken by lust and fought to the near-death. Maybe you think of him as some black-furred mole who, scooped out of his lair, can only flail blindly, struggling stupidly for purchase in the light of day.

But I see him sweating furiously for a language, any language, a system to hook him into a code of meaning that is neither cryptic nor provisional, but historic. Others see the impulsiveness, the sudden tantrums, the crazy risks, but I see a man trying to catapult himself into the universal language of cause-and-effect, into the company of the revolutionaries who preceded him and those who will come after. That he could act we agree; that he had agency, well, history cut him off in the middle of a speech.

— Shifting Points of View —

From the Mennonites' point of view, the *makhnoshchyna* was a reign of terror carried out by fiends in human form: drunken robber bands; rapists and pillagers; lawless hordes of outlaws made up of the criminal classes and rabble who left behind a "gory wake of death and destruction." It was a savagery, C. Henry Smith has written hyperbolically, "almost unequalled among any civilized people in modern history." It had a face and a stench, this savagery: the crazed yelp of the bloodied peasants who dragged the girls out of their hiding places, and raped them over and over again before hacking them to pieces (*hacking them to pieces?*); the fiery ruins, the bleating livestock. "It was like a wolfhunt" wrote Joseph Height. "No one was safe." People fleeing their homes were shot down in the street, those hiding in bales of hay were blindly bayonetted by brigands furiously stabbing at them in the dark, and, while their menfolk lay dying and the church fell in flames, the women and girls were forced (odd detail this) "to dance with the murderers."

Compared to this "social revolution," the occupation of the region by Austro-German troops in the summer of 1918 had been a "pleasant interlude" for the Mennonites. But it was an interlude during which, from the Ukrainians' point of view, the peasantry suffered a terrible punishment from the "military and landed castes [read Mennonite farmers], who professed neutrality in the war but looked forward to the restoration of the czarist regime." Peter Arshinov, the anarchist chronicler, wrote of the "colossal and horrifying" economic pillage of the Ukrainian villages by the occupiers, how they carried off everything — wheat, livestock, poultry, eggs — all in such quantities that the means of transportation was not sufficient. I am left thinking of how those who bear the brunt of violence always tell it the same way: Russians, Germans, Ukrainians, they all have chickens that they always lose.

## — Legend Begets Legend —

It is said that, after the destruction of the *Sich*, the defeated Cossacks of Zaporozhia built a monastery in the marshes farther off. They became monks and dressed and lived as the peasants. Eventually they built a cathedral that rose into the heavens below which their horses used to graze. They wanted to build a monument to liberty: "Our sabres have been forced from our hands," the novelist Oles Honchar records, "but the spirit of liberty and . . . our resistance will manifest [themselves] in this creation in the steppes forever." They built it and hung a great bell.

Then came the time of the *makhnoshchyna* and the anarchists of Huliai-Pole swooped down upon the cathedral, worshipped at it and decided to haul away its great bell. Across the silty Skrabny marshes they pulled their purloined treasure behind teams of oxen groaning in their wooden yokes. But the sturdy cart could not bear the weight of the "cossack copper." The bell fell through, down into the deep marshy pool. They say that it tolled for seven days and seven nights before it reached the bottom.

*Why did your people kill my people?*

I know now what Batko means to you, looming so darkly in your folktales. He is the disruption of the natural order, chaotic and stupid rage without historical memory. His violence is bestial. It has no right. It goes nowhere. It is sterile and without issue, except, of course, that it has produced your grief.

## — Notebook —

A snow-slicked backroad winds from the drab stubbled fields (Manitoba in November) around a clump of bony poplar. There is a farm here, a poor scrabble of land, narrow and stony and good-for-nothing, where everything happened, and nothing.

Once upon a time there had been a great jungle of bush along the creek and you swam naked among the little fish. But it's all stripped now, dead, played out. Out there under the shopping mall were the fields where you snared rabbits, built a little fire, boiled up tea in a tin pail. There was Grandfather, planted two-footed on this land, hard and wild and driven. Beyond the crude carpentry of the garden gate his cherry orchard is gnarled, sour-fruited. His house burned in flames behind his back, and he held his young dead wife still in his heart while his second one sold the farm, his spindle-shanked body not yet cold in its grave. "There's nothing here you would want," she told you, his grieving grandson. But I find something in the log barn: horse collars, gristly from winters, a cream separator, and the old man's *kozhukh*, with its thick woolly lining spilling out on the lapels, its natty flap pockets and row of buttons, none missing, as if he had left it at a tailor's and never gone back for it.

The coat excites me and I take pictures of it; it could be *my* grandfather's. And there it is again, my busybody's need to link these stories, the Menno and Ukrainian, oblivious to the Germanness of this cold barn, the language of the curses that built it, the low-lander heft of the shoulders that held the sheepskin up. Maybe it wasn't even Grandfather's. He never did tell his stories, or the ones he told were made up. He had four Russian stories. One: his grandfather went down to Odessa to see the sea. Two: the workless Ukrainian peasants were wild and drunken. Three: the barking dogs had different barks, depending on who their master was: Ukrainian, Jewish, or Mennonite. Four: the Jewish pedlar who travelled from village to village brought the news: Jacob's died, Cornelius and Clara are getting married.

You do not even look. The old man is not there. You go back to the typewriter. He is hopping between the keys.


## PART THREE

### — Menno Versions of Revolution —

First come the Bolsheviks, then comes genocide, the Mennonite people dying of typhoid, cholera, influenza, starvation, and execution a mere year later. There is no other news between the revolution and the dying, no mention of manifestos or newspapers, programs or decrees, nothing of land reform or workers' councils or women's suffrage, no slogans or songs or eulogies, only death. Or, as the poet writes: "Ruin, ruin, ruin" . . . in the place of Menno order. One day you have money, a plump wife, thick crops in the fields and apples tumbling like coins in the orchard, and the next day your wife is dead, your brothers scattered, your children starving, the apple tree limbs broken like sticks.

Where there was something now there is nothing. Or: where there was once Kornelson's sturdy house there is now lumber for the offices of the People's Committees. There is a pile of firewood where Neufeld had his apple trees. And Kornelson hanging from the rafters of his barn amid the ghosts of his horses. The poet, John Weier: "You see the Russian wisdom, the People's wisdom."

There is no more soap, underwear, razors. Your hair is matted and lice-ridden, like ours. Your boots were purloined long ago and now you hobble around in cloth bindings — *like a muzhik!*

We move into your house — three families in Dirksen's home — and sit in the dark because, although we have lightbulbs, there is no power. Remember how the rooms used to glow with light and you never lacked for fuel? We've torn down Warkentin's house and hauled the material away for one of our own villages. J. Toews's house we've turned into a hospital for degenerate war veterans, Reimer's general store is a Red club house, Schroeder's stable houses the collective's cows, and Bartel's summer house is a garbage dump. Russian huts cover the playground and in the church, crawling on all fours, are the orphans and little cripples, all sorts of pitiable, human derelicts. This is the fate of the once prosperous Mennonite village of Orloff as described in 1938.

Sterility and barrenness. Nothing grows anymore because no one goes out to plough. It doesn't matter, you see. Everything has changed, so *b* no longer necessarily follows *a*. You go out to plough, *we* come along and take your team, your seed grain for our own collective fields. You don't have to bother anymore, see? "Necessity was nowhere," writes Rudy Wiebe. "Gone."

In the fall of 1918 the Soviet Food Commissariat granted the "worker columns" the right to collect food from the farmers. These forays were carried out with ruthless violence on a grand scale: in 1918 the requisitioners collected over half a million tons, in 1919 almost two million tons, and in 1920 more than 5.7 million tons. Certainly one of the largest wholesale looting operations in history.

Yes, but how would *you* have fed the workers and the soldiers?

How a Mennonite knows the cosmic order has been over-turned: a "Russian" yokel has moved into his house from the barn and sleeps in his bed. He snores. The *schlunga*.

# — Notebook —

Tell me how I should see this. If I say that the vengeance of the oppressed is no tea party, you will say such language is a self-deception designed to hide the speaker (me) from the truth. Truth is non-violence, nakedness, you say, and the willingness to risk paradox and the endless reopening of dogma's closure.

And if I say that revolution frees the oppressed (Ukrainians) from the interminable recycling of the here-and-now, you will say that the here-and-now is precisely where you want to live: enough with the hollow God-figures on their astral plane; the future is always empty.

And if I say that the oppressed need no more martyrs but actors (Makhno), you will tell me about the doomed Russian poet Marina Tsvetayeva who, in an inflexible act of self-knowledge, hanged herself, and who are we to judge this useless? Perhaps it is only the "intimate" and "immediate" act—not the grand gesture played to History—that makes a difference? But I will say that it is to the intimate and immediate scale of things that the scullery maids and cowherds have always been condemned.

The peasants know only the acts that have no audience and the deeds that circulate no farther than the folktales they murmur together. It isn't that the future is empty, it's that there isn't one at all: time folds back on itself for them and traps them in their own beginnings. Give us, they say, an ending.

Talk to me, be my friend. Drag me away from this dispute. Makhno is mouldering in his grave. Tsvetayeva hanged light as a rag on her rope. I feel giddy with argument. Embrace me.

Nursing his grievances against his brutal masters, the Makhno runt dreams not of being a pure flame of anything, but of being a *thug*. A thug in the woods with his buddies, smacking their fat lips over bottles of vodka, scratching at their crotches as they schemed horse-thievery and rape, imagining they were (ha ha) Cossacks.

*"Fighting? That cowardly pipsqueak? With a peasant army, you say? Don't make me laugh. He's probably holed up in Dibrovka Forest north of here with a few buddies and their whores, quaking every time he hears a leaf fall."* Snapper Loewen, son of Mennonite landowner, head of a mounted posse organized with approval of occupying Austrian district commander, hoping to capture Batko Makhno.

Later, though, Snapper is forced to revise his views. He is in Makhno's company, when Makhno is clearly in charge of the situation, the glint of his dark eyes and the absolute self-control of his half-smile compensate for the boyishness of his slight frame and fleshy lips. Snapper realizes "this was no sneaky little *khokhol* making sheep's eyes at an innocent girl [but] a man primed to deal instant destruction, like the weapons poised at his elbow."

Makhno is meeting with his anarchist comrades early on in the revolution in Huliai-Pole. Here is the Menno fantasy of how a Ukrainian anarchist makes the revolution: the punk has become a man. You can tell he's a man because his voice flares in anger, his eyes are tigerish and steely, his speech is fiery and full of vulgarities (fat-asses; stupid buggers; wipe the sweat off my balls), and he bangs the table a lot. His aim in the revolution is to impose his will on other men. The measure of his success is that his comrades, weaker men, do not even know until it's over that he has had his way with them.

Near you, close enough to press my shoulder into your arm, I don't feel womanly. I feel chaste, the woman still to be touched. No marriage bed for us. For all your evocation of the "slavic wildness" in me, I feel only your recoil as your limbs curl up in some fetal memory of perfect solitude. You didn't always want it to be this way. After all, you made two babies on your wife's body and spilled (okay, uselessly) into others'. Let me be the virgin, tending your perpetual fire. I will never marry. It will be unlucky.

You are watery, you say. I think of a shoreline so far inland its lapping lip scarcely feels the tug of the tide. I think of the boatman on his skiff (this is a dream in which you have all the parts), heaving himself seaward on the point of a pole dug deep into the soft clay of the riverbed, stirring up its yellowish grit, while I stand on the bank waving a handkerchief. I wring my hands as you grow smaller and smaller, casting spells for a fair breeze that brings you back to shore where I can find you. I'll find you dripping seaweed, shivering, licking your own skin for salt.

## — Enter the Ukrainian servants: The Blockhead and the Slut —

In a passionate outburst to her young Mennonite charges, the Russian (Ukrainian?) teacher in *Lost in the Steppe*, Varvara Pavlovna, excoriates them and their parents for their many unkindnesses towards her—"because I am Russian." I can imagine her shaking with the injury of it, at the same time determined to answer back to the Mennonite community's disdain of her. "You are the foreigners here, you are our guests," she reminds them, reordering what must be to them the "natural" scheme of things: the "German" as proprietor.

In fact, as she herself admits, the Ukrainians who worked the German land had never owned it. They had always worked *for* someone, as far back as their collective memory could take them. There was this one thing that distinguished the Mennonites from her own people and tore at her pride: "Your sons and daughters don't go into service."

If there is a Ukrainian literature about the culture of the "house nigger" on the estates of southern Ukraine, I've not heard about it. The Canadian prairie narrative that I grew up with was of the Ukrainian immigrant woman as cleaning lady. If you wanted someone who would get at the goop behind the stove and polish the hardwood floors by hand, and be really grateful for the work, hire a *stara baba* [Ukr. old woman; disrespectful].

The world view this represented was irritating but not insufferable. By the time we got around to telling the anecdote, the *stara baba's* kids had housekeepers of their own. Being "in service" was the sacrifice the immigrating generation made for the ones to come. It wasn't a caste stigma. Yet it seems that the sheer predictability of the Ukrainian showing up in Mennonite tales as houseservant or hired hand is a reflection of the fact that this is probably the only contact rich Germans had with Ukrainian peasants, generation after generation.

It does seem to be the case, however, that Mennonites did generally pay and feed their hired help more generously than other landlords. They offered wages as much as fifty to seventy percent above the average, but expected hard work in exchange. Many of the Ukrainians took advantage of the arrangement as a kind of apprenticeship in husbandry. "Barin, I will be busy with my own land now. I have learned a lot. Thank you." There are stories, too, that Mennonite farmers and their servants sat down at table together.

But for the most part the Ukrainian servant worked best under threat of violence: "The Russians just need more thrashings, only more thrashings, then they will become tame." Tamed, they know to doff their caps when the master's guests drive into the yard of the great house, or, like the rheumy-eyed and loyal Anton in *My Harp Is Turned to Mourning*, "absolutely" refuse to enter the house, preferring life in the stable alongside the animals, stinking the same as they. Anton was born a serf and presumably the habits of freedom come hard. "[He] received no regular wages and had never asked for any. But his devotion to the . . . family was total."

Untamed, the Ukrainian blockhead gets blindingly drunk and careers, legs all tangled, along the fence until he collapses in a boozy heap and falls asleep. Half-awakened by agitprop, he loses all restraint, strikes out blindly. Or, drunk on revolution, he swaggers around the property, like Escha in Wiebe's *Blue Mountains of China*, trying out the master's bed and blankets when he should have remembered that "Russians belonged in the barn."

As for the Ukrainian female servant in the same households, she is a slut, the sloe-eyed, exotic beauty in the starched white uniform. She drives the sons crazy with the suggestion of her availability, "touchable for the reaching," the plumped-out shoulders, breasts and hips under the white underdress, the opportunity of her presence in the barn or stable or cook house.

"Blessed saviour make me pure make me pure." Thus the prayerful inner voice of the young, tumid Jakob Friesen, in *Blue Mountains of China*, in a vain effort to suppress his maddening desire for the Ukrainian wench (she is nameless) who fucks Escha the Ukrainian blockhead on a regular basis in the hayloft. Jakob stumbles upon them, alerted by the girl's laugh, and sees, as if from between his fingers, the swirling dust, a long naked leg, the half-shadowed breast, the "half-gilded, gigantic columns" of Escha. Jakob reels out of the barn in a fit of disgusted excitement. "You pigs you stinking naked pigs, in my father's barn you naked pigs!"

Here is then the contamination of Mennonite virtue (in this case the patriarch's real estate) by the primal Slavic body. But we know what's going to happen anyway: into the black and bottomless vortex of the whore's beguiling torpor (spiritual as well as physical), Jakob is going to be sucked like flotsam off the edge of his own lust, this black thing squatting at the edge of his consciousness. *The devil made him do it.*

The still-nameless girl and Escha, fully-clothed this time, literally dance the Mennonite boy into their carnal circle. The author, Rudy Wiebe, imagines it as a kind of steppe dance of the seven veils, the girl in heavy skirts and knee-high boots, slithering along the barn floor, swaying her hips at Jakob, "her eyes all fire," while Escha sings and claps, urging them on. Jakob, whose body is plodding and graceless, begins in spite of himself *make me pure make me pure* to respond. He is circling her as her body pivots in the bend of his arm. Her breasts thrust out with each fling of her arm, her blouse slips down, her black hair falls away, exposing the "domes of her violent breasts" (violent?), her lips swell in "red, terrible beauty," and he is "growing immense beyond possibility" (!) when Escha joins the dance and the two men circle "to her core" as though in melt-down.

This isn't rape, this is communal pleasure, earthy and ritual, that only the Ukrainians, alas, know how to enjoy. When Jakob goes looking for the girl in the hayloft again, she gurgles and rings with laughter from the kingdom of light; he, feeling her hand upon him, slips into the "unknown and bottomless" darkness.

— Notebook —

Isn't it interesting, you ask, that *slut* and *lust* share the same letters?

There she is again, the (Ukrainian) slut.

We were talking of them, the Menno boy and the Ukrainian girl. It made utter sense to you that this boy, raised in the fear of the Lord to "know" the Menno women only in marriage and baby-making, is present here in this physical moment of the blood risen up in him, and here is the Ukrainian girl whose significance is that you will never marry her. *Simply fine, physical fucking without guilt,* and so you have her. When you return to her, she'll still be there.

## — There Is a Variation—The Ukrainian Revolutionary Slut —

In Al Reimer's *My Harp Is Turned To Mourning,* she is first presented as Marusya (no surname), the sullen houseservant who, in bed with the young master, August Bock, metamorphoses into a sex-hellion, "an elemental force that swept him to dizzying heights of passion." Nevertheless, he complains. She is so furious in her love-making, she frightens him. With her wild threshings and savage kisses, she was more beast than woman, "as though she wanted to destroy him." In fact, the more he thinks about this, the more he understands the true nature of their relations: she hates him. How else explain her heartless violation of his body "as though *he* were the hired whore. . . . The rotten bitch!"

It's he who is raped? He does protest too much. Tell me: how does the Menno wife make love? in her thick cotton shift, her hands curled in little fists, her eyes closed against the pitch dark?

Then Marusya runs away, yes! And is transformed again, into Chaika, the revolutionary bitch-cum-guerrillera dressed like a man in wide Cossack pants and a military cape. She rides like a man, smells rank like a man too long sleeping away from his own bed, and takes lovers like a man used to the convenience of trollops. Having polluted Mennonite sexual purity on the Bock estate, she now corrupts her young male followers, cradling them on her "lean bosom," smirking with satisfaction as she "swallows lovers like a snake swallowing an egg." Finally she meets her libidinal match in the young Nikolai, a renegade Mennonite, who pounds away at her until, "grudgingly" submissive, she pleads for him to stop. (But not so submissive as to have an orgasm, no. Does she stop fucking precisely in order *not* to come?)

Meanwhile, the Ukrainian male revolutionary, Makhno, has desires of his own, namely Katya, the young Mennonite beauty he had worshipped from a distance since his boyhood working for her father. The vision of her unattainable loveliness, "his lovely pure angel," had consoled him in the long, dark days of his imprisonment. With his mind running riot, "caress[ing] petal by petal the aching mystery of her," he masturbates himself to exhaustion in dismal mimicry of the tender urgency to stroke *her*, his smooth *golubka*, his little pigeon. When he sees her again, it is the revolution and he is handsome in a well-tailored uniform and elegant boots. He never touches her but he hovers, staring insatiably, then suddenly snatches one of her handkerchiefs and, "grinning a ghastly grin," disappears.

And how does the Mennonite object of Ukrainian desire respond? Her admirer is a "little monster," a "beastly little man," a "brazen little thief," and so on, taking whatever he wanted (but not her) "like a wild Cossack."

Reimer misses completely the possibility that this "wild Cossack" *excited* Katya who, unlike her author, may have been able to imagine the mutuality of Ukrainian-Mennonite desire. Perhaps that "brazen little thief" was an instance of her own body's revolt against her husband's lovemaking: a blond Christian husband, say, who would never dream of asking his wife for the pleasure he took in the barn with Marusya, her arms wrapped around his hips, sucking him to kingdom come, his tongue lapping at her lips. Makhno himself had only imagined a big, rich farmer mounting her "grunting in the dark."

This is an interesting political economy of cross-cultural desire in a time of scarcity. The Mennonite male desires the Ukrainian female, and may have her. The Ukrainian male desires the Mennonite woman but may not have her. There is no notion of the specific desire of the Ukrainian woman—she'll take anybody—nor of the dignity of marriage between Ukrainians. As for the girls of the Ukrainian village, compared to the comely Mennonite maidens of the German farms, they are "cows." The Mennonite women, of course, are wives; their bodies signify not their own pleasure or anyone else's but the conduit of patriarchal lineage. Sluts or mothers, all the women in these villages seem fraught in their flesh while the men dance around them, out of their skins.

> *. . . the long*
> *arm of love on my shoulder and me rehearsing my disappearance*
> *from the body*

> — Patrick Friesen,
> "blasphemous wheel"

Right up to your marriage bed you would not know your bride except through the Law, the Word. You brought the soulful love of the bridegroom who, twitching and shuddering, would have to break the taboo. *Thou shalt not! Touch!*

*Nor shalt thou Sing! Dance!* We do them for you, *fall into the flesh*, tune up our fiddles under the waxing moon, clutch our partner by the hip and bounce off the barn walls, shrieking out our exuberance. You call it "jungle music" and you call us "carefree brutes" and yet you want to follow us there, into the darkness, to have the prayer knocked out of you by these smooth, sunbrowned Ukrainian arms around your neck that pull you down. Tongue to tongue, fingers entwined, belly to belly, we will print our body's memory on you and in shame and greed you will lie with your relenting bride.

*. . . the freedom to go unobserved,*
*in a thicket or in a cave gouged from a hillside*
*the freedom of idleness to breathe*
*in and out the freedom of his heart*

— Patrick Friesen,
"Remington"

## — Notebook —

You were talking of freedom, but I think of the freedom of the body unhinged from intellect, the body unhinged from the church. You write, "you had to get out, you had to get out, be alone somewhere, be left alone . . ." Your body resists the distraction of theology and instruction in order to flame, alone and sequestered, in a moment of pure feeling.

With you, though, feeling is embodied. That's the sensuousness. You want to live in the flesh that is the spirit's own sinewed arm.

But *she* wants to get away, melt her flesh down to release her spirit mired in this material muck and go join the revolution. You haul down memory into your body. Her body is nothing but.

Didn't it ever occur to you that, if we danced and sang and fucked, it was to shake ourselves loose of our requisitioned flesh and leap out, free?

## — Epilogue —

What a guy he was, eh? Out on the battlefield: now you see him, now you don't. Throw a noose around him and he slips out before you can draw it tight. He's small and lithe, like a dancer. He dances on the steppe. Foxy.

Are there women in this picture? He drinks prodigiously and flies into awesome rages. Who will bed such a man? Does he dream of Mennonite flesh as he lies wounded and feverish in his camp bed? It is only when he is dressed in uniform, in knee-high boots, when he arrives uninvited with an entourage of warriors, that he dares to look straight into the eyes of the daughters and lets them know that if he doesn't take them it is because he chooses not to.

He is mine. While I lay under you, bearing the weight of your guilty excitement on my belly, your ragged breath in my mouth, I expelled your sticky seed into the cold: did you not know that I was barren? I wasn't *there*. I was on my way to Batko.

# BELGRADE

*H*e is so young, a nestling, escaped from his parents' home to go striding here beside me through cool and foggy streets that twist and turn away from Republic Square, loping on long, thin legs in blue jeans along Makedonska, his knapsack hanging on one shoulder, his buddies in the doorway of the Kinoteka.

We've come to see "Flesh," a Paul Morrissey flick. I have vague memories of Andy Warhol movies in a cinema at midnight on Yonge Street in Toronto thirty years ago. I remember the daring-ness of sitting in the dark space flickered by light leaking from Warhol's basement pallor and the sweaty, corpulent glory of Divine. Dead now. But the boys are all excited, hunkered down in the seats, eons away from the sadness of Belgrade. He falls asleep, his head resting on his left shoulder, away from me. I want to pull him over, tilt him onto my breast.

After the movie, the boys are hungry. I buy his buddy a can of beer, him a box of cookies—their choices—in the little grocery not far from the Kinoteka. He is so thin. He eats abominably; it makes him "interesting," he says, not to care about food. But when I take him and his girlfriend to lunch one afternoon at "Pod Lepom," he wolfs down soup and salad, chicken Kiev and fries and beer. The girlfriend pokes at salad, high, apparently, on heroin. They have quarrelled. I am serene.

They are holding hands and I am walking behind them, two

pairs of long, lean legs, slender striplings. A long walk, late at night away from the hotel and into the gardens behind Saint Mark's. He brings out a joint and blows smoke overhead into the naked chestnut branches. At her end of the bench the girlfriend twitches, taps her heels, while he and I lean back together against the broken slats and talk about Hesse. I haven't thought about Herman Hesse in years and have no idea what I think.

He and I have an entire Sunday, with no sign of the girlfriend. We swing off the handstraps in the clattering buses that take us on the itinerary he has chosen. We sit on a park bench on Ada Island and eat ice cream in the weak sunshine. Move to a little sidewalk café for cappuccino, Bosnian folksongs on a boombox, curled brown leaves crunched under our feet. I hand over the money. My cavalier, he runs the errands. In Saint Mark's cavernous space we stand before the brass tray of votive candles while he genuflects and solemnly kisses the wax stem of his sputtering taper. How does he know how to do this, I wonder, this adorable hippy flotsam of ex-Yugoslavia?

He has a way, mid-stride, of releasing his fine hair out of its hairband and shaking it loose so that it flies in the air like a fan, perhaps for my admiration, and later I will wish I had reached out to catch it between my open fingers. Instead, I stare at his perfect ear. It is delectable, pierced with a silver cross.

I have to make a call to Paris. We stop in the deserted post office in Vase Carapica Street, take a booth. He is standing in the narrow doorway, holding the door open. I dial the numbers but nothing happens. I turn for help, and he leans in towards the phone, dialing for me. Standing between his two arms, I feel small, pliant, quiet. His head is above and to the side of me. I could tilt mine up and kiss his bearded chin. I concentrate on the sleek whiteness of his neck. That is where I will kiss him when we stand at the departure gates and I sense rather than see his long body curving over me.

On our last night we meet at the opera house, after the performance. How long has he been standing there in the portico?

Over the bobbing heads in the lobby I see him out in the cold, looking at me. He is simply there and I see him. He chooses the Kino Klub. We enter its high-ceilinged space foggy with cigarette smoke and skip down the staircase to the beat of Bruce Springsteen singing "Dancing in the Dark." For a few startling seconds, my private life, elsewhere, before him, has reached out and grabbed me out of dark and sorrowing Belgrade.

But here is this Serbian boy licking the coffee spoon, his long fingers curling the hair behind his ear, telling me there is nothing interesting about him and his life in Serbia. "The truth is gone out of here, out of this world. Only the enemy is telling the truth. I am losing ground under my feet. Every day is the same. I get this terrible feeling that I am who I am now, and it will always be like this. Serbia is the worst place to live in the universe, it doesn't matter who is the fucking president."

Months later there will be a couple of letters, written from his parents' house south of Belgrade, in unsteady English and unfaltering despair. His narrowed world is subsiding into deeper gloom as soldiers and tanks rattle down the highways to Kosovo and the Albania insurgents. Flowers pressed into the pages of his books make him think of death, he says. And his own poetry, eked out from his sleepy brain, disgusts him.

I want to lift my hand from the table, uncurl my fingers, tug at his monkish beard, drag a finger along his lower lip. This is, after all, good-bye. "Why are you so interested in us? Why do you keep coming here to Belgrade?" he asks, and I keep my hands in my lap. Oh my doomed darling.

He is leaning over the table, his chin in both hands, his face open, guileless, his eyes a wide stare of concentration as though to memorize this moment. Perhaps, much later, if someday he should live in peace and write his poems, my story will be in his. But that is the future, beyond me to tell. My story is this moment, a receding point of light in a contracting history, what is left of memory and a fury of hapless love.

# SOURCES AND BIBLIOGRAPHY

## Preface

Morgan, Robin. *The Demon Lover: On the Sexuality of Terrorism*. New York: W. W. Norton & Company, 1990.

———. "Goodbye To All That." In *Voices From Women's Liberation*. New York: New American Library, 1971.

Edelson, Miriam. "Letting Go of the Union Label: The Feminization of a Macho Myth." *This Magazine* (October/November 1991).

Wilson, Elizabeth. "A New Romanticism?" In *The Left and the Erotic*. Edited by Eileen Phillips. London: Lawrence & Wishart, 1983.

Phillips, Eileen. "Introduction: Libertarianism, 'Egotism' and Liberation." In *The Left and the Erotic*.

## Mississippi Dreaming and The Collaborators

As experiments with memorabilia, "Mississippi Dreaming" and "The Collaborators" have their sources in my diaries, journals and private correspondence, as well as in secondary sources I was reading along the way in the history of the war in Vietnam and the period of the Junta in Greece (1967–1974).

Dylan, Bob. "Leopard-Skin Pill-box Hat." From *Blonde on Blonde*. New York: Columbia Records, 1965.

Emboldened by the experiment, I ranged further afield to contextualize the stories about Vasyl Stus, K, and the Mennonites in Ukraine.

## Inside the Copper Mountain

Stus, Vasyl. "Hide Within." Trans. Marko Carynnyk. In *The Writer and Human Rights*. Edited by the Toronto Arts Group for Human Rights. Toronto: Lester & Orpen Dennys, 1983.

———. "All the same there is nothing sweeter." "And there will be parting enough for two." Trans. Volodymyr Hruszkewycz. In *Spirits of the Age: Poets of Conscience*. Edited by Mona Adilman. Kingston: Quarry Press, 1989.

———. "Leap over the precipice." "Tell me that you love me." "So that gathered into yourself." "Through Oblivion." "For We Are Very Few." Trans. Jaropolk Lassowsky. In *Vasyl Stus: Selected Poems*. Munich: The Ukrainian Free University, 1987.

———. "Lysty Vasilia Stusa Do Viry Vovk [ Letters to Vera Vovk]." *Suchasnist* 9 (1989). My translation.

———. "Lyst Do Syna [Letter to his Son]." *Suchasnist* 1 (1989). My trans-
lation.
———. "Lysty Vasilia Stusa Do Syna i Druzhyny [Letters to his Wife and
Son]." *Suchasnist* 9 (1989). My translation.
———. "Z Taborovoho Zoshyta [From the Camp Notebook]." *Suchasnist*
11 (1983). My translation.
———. "J'Accuse." Trans. Jaropolk Lassowsky. From "Biographical
Sketch of Vasyl Stus." In *Vasyl Stus: Selected Poems*.
The lines "Like a star . . ." (my translation) are from an untitled poem pub-
lished in vol. 1, book 1, of Stus's collected works, *Tvory u chotyriokh
tomakh, shesty knyhakh* (Lviv 1994).

For other accounts of Stus's life in the camps and his death, including Boris
Penson's reminiscence, I read:
Stus, Vasyl. "Biographical Sketch of Vasyl Stus." Trans. Jaropolk
Lassowsky. In *Vasyl Stus: Selected Poems*.
Also useful were the recollections published in *Suchasnist*, especially those
of Serhiy Soldatov and of an anonymous fellow prisoner—"The last
time I saw Stus was in 1981?"—as collected by Anna-Halia Horbach,
*Suchasnist* 5 (1986).

For my translated accounts of Stus's posthumous fate I read:
Shovkoshytnyi, Volodymyr. "Narode Miy, Do tebe ia shche vernu [My
People, It Is To You I Am Returning]." *Ukraina* (January 1990).
Chernilevskyi, Stanislav. "Napevne, Ty taky ne tut, Taky ne tut [You're
Not Really Here, Not Really Here]." *Ukraina* (n.d.).
"The Return." *Suchasnist* 4 (1989).

Sources for my translations of three reminiscences:
Kotsiubensky, Mykhailyna. "U Svichadi Pam'iati [In the Mirror of
Memory]" *Ukraina* (June 1990). They include her quotation of a line of
Stus's poetry, "You aren't really here, not really here."
Svitlychna, Nadia. "Pro Vasylia Stusa [About Vasyl Stus]." In *Vasyl Stus v
zhytti, tvorchosti ta otsinkakh suchasnykiv [ Vasyl Stus's Life and Art and the
Appraisal of His Contemporaries]*." Baltimore: Smoloskyp Publishers, 1987.
Heifetz, Mykhailo. "V ukrainskyi poezii teper bil'shoho nema [The Last of
His Kind in Ukrainian Poetry]." In *Vasyl Stus v zhytti, tvorchosti ta
otsinkakh suchasnykiv [Vasyl Stus's Life and Art and the Appraisal of His
Contemporaries]*."

Other accounts of the dissidence of the "Sixties people" appear in:
*Ukrainian Herald IV*. Munich (n.d.).
*Dissent in Ukraine: The Ukrainian Herald Issue 6*. Edited and trans. by Lesya
Jones and Bohdan Yasen. Baltimore: Smoloskyp Publishers, 1977.
Plyushch, Leonid. *History's Carnival: A Dissident's Autobiography*. Edited and

trans. by Marko Carynnyk. New York: Harcourt Brace Jovanovich, 1979.

Chornovil, Viacheslav. *The Chornovil Papers.* (n.p. n.d.).

Osadchy, Mykhaylo. *Cataract.* Trans. Marko Carynnyk. New York: Harcourt Brace Jovanovich, 1976.

Marchenko, Anatol. *My Testimony.* London: Sceptre Books, 1987.

———. *For This Was I Born.* Edited and trans. by Yuri Shymko. Toronto: UCRAINCA Research Institute, 1973.

Shifron, Avraham. "A patch of hummocky land." In *The First Guidebook to Prisons and Concentration Camps of the Soviet Union.* New York: Bantam, 1982.

Horbal, Mykola. "Parts of an Hourglass." *Ukrainian Weekly* (September 11, 1988).


## The Masked Man in Warsaw

To understand the nature of post-war Polish Communism and its effect on writers I read:

Toranska, Teresa. *Them: Stalin's Polish Puppets.* New York: HarperCollins, 1988. (This was also the source for the reference to Party Secretary Stefan Staszewski.)

Milosz, Czeslaw. *The History of Polish Literature.* Berkeley: University of California Press, 1983. (Especially helpful for details about Jerzy Andrzejewski.)

———. *The Captive Mind.* Available in many editions.

Andrzejewski, Jerzy. *Ashes and Diamonds.* Harmondsworth: Penguin, 1980.

Some details about censorship in K's circles are available in:

*The Black Book of Polish Censorship.* Edited by Jane Leftwich Curry. New York: Vintage, 1984.


Other "taxonomists" of the Communist intellectual:

Raina, P. K. *Political Opposition in Poland 1954–1977.* London: Poets and Painters Press, 1978.

Michnik, Adam. *Letters From Prison.* Berkeley: University of California Press, 1985.

Brandys, Kazimierz. *A Warsaw Diary 1978–1981.* London: Chatto & Windus, 1984.

Wat, Aleksander. *My Century: The Odyssey of a Polish Intellectual.* New York: Norton, 1990.


Details about Warsaw in the aftermath of World War II were provided by:

Karol, K.S. *Visa For Poland.* London: MacGibbon & Kee, 1959.

Gunther, John. *Behind the Curtain.* New York: Harper & Bros., 1949.

Yugoslav Communist Milovan Djilas includes a description of devastated

Warsaw in:

Djilas, Milovan. *Rise and Fall*. New York: Harvest/HBJ, 1985.

Poland's experience during World War II is massively documented, including in:

Zawodny, J.K. *Nothing But Honour*. Stanford: Hoover Institution Press,
1979. (It deals with the Warsaw uprising.)

For additional details I referred to:

Borger, Julian. "Memories from the Ghetto." *Manchester Guardian Weekly*
(April 25 1993). The lines of poetry beginning "Qui n'a pas vu les
ruines" are from Paul Eluard's "Dans Varsovie la Ville Fantastique" and
are quoted in this article.

Craig, Gordon. "Schreibt und Farschreibt!" *The New York Review of Books*
(April 10 1986).

The quote from Reinhard Heydrich at the Wansee Conference was taken
from the film, *Wansee Conference*, directed by Heinz Schirk. Rear Guard
Productions, 1987.

Zbigniew Herbert interview. *The Partisan Review*, 4 (1987).

The lines of poetry beginning "Un-human Poland, howling with boredom,"
are from Adam Wazyk's "Poem for Adults," reprinted in a variety of
sources; I found it in *Bitter Harvest*, ed. Edmund Stillman. New York:
Praeger, 1959.

The ditty, "Bridge to the right etc." was sung to me by Bohdan Nebesio and
Ania Andrusieczko in Edmonton who learned it in school in Poland in
the 1960s.

Janina Bauman's memoir of "Polish October" was published as:

*A Dream of Belonging*. London: Virago, 1988.

Other details of the period, including Adam Michnik's court appearances
and speeches, come from:

Karpinski, Jakub. *Countdown: The Polish Upheavals of 1956, 1968, 1970, 1976,
1980...* New York: Karz-Cohl, 1984.

Milan Kundera's *The Joke* (several editions) is the source for his quote,
"They love their bodies . . ."

Details of the cultural thaw of 1956 are from an interview in Edmonton in
1996 with Jan Tereszczenko.

Orlos, Kazimierz. "Barbed Wire Fox." *Index on Censorship* (March 1984).

Comprehensive material about the Solidarity period provided in:

Ascherson, Neal. *The Polish August*. Harmondsworth: Penguin, 1982.Garton
Ash, Timothy. *The Polish Revolution*. New York: Random House, 1985.

Former Solidarity activists interviews. *Konspira: Solidarity Underground*.
Edited by Maciej Lopinski, Marcin Moskit, and Mariusz Wilk.

Berkeley: University of California Press, 1990.
A fictionalized treatment of the "verification committee" process is in:
Nowakowski, Marek. *The Canary*. New York: Dial Press 1984.

The papers collected by Peter Potichnyj in *Poland and Ukraine: Past and Present* (Toronto: CIUS Press, 1980) were helpful in understanding that history.
Nikolai Gogol's *Taras Bulba* (many editions) and Henryk Sienkiewicz's swash-buckling novel, *With Fire and Sword*, about the Polish-Cossack wars, also proved inspirational.

Details about K have been changed to protect his identity.

## Lord, History Falls Through the Cracks

The title is from the poem, "flicker and hawk," from:
Friesen, Patrick. *Flicker and Hawk*. Winnipeg: Turnstone, 1987.
Also by Patrick Friesen:
——— . "Nestor Makhno: Anarchist." In *in the lands i am*. Winnipeg: Turnstone, 1976. (For the lines "Makhno lies long dead.")
——— . "Blasphemous Wheel." In *Blasphemer's Wheel*. Winnipeg: Turnstone, 1994. (For the lines ". . . the long arm of love.")
——— . "Remington." In *Unearthly Horses*. Winnipeg: Turnstone, 1984. (For the lines ". . . the freedom to go unobserved.")
Also useful: Zbigniew Herbert interview. *The Partisan Review*, 4 (1987).
Interview by Robert Enright. *Prairie Fire*, 1, 13 (Spring 1992). (Dedicated to the work of Friesen, this is the source of the line, "It goes mouth to ear, body to body.")
I have also relied on private correspondence.

For the general history of Mennonites and for their period in Ukraine I read:
Smith, C. Henry. *The Story of the Mennonites*. Berne, Ind.: Mennonite Book Concern, 1945. (Also the source of the Bishop of Culm's complaint and the anecdote about the steppe wolves.)
Urry, James. *None But Saints: The Transformation of Mennonite Life in Russia 1789–1889*. Winnipeg: Hypernion, 1989. (Also the source of the illustration of "a typical Mennonite farm" and the declaration of the teacher Peter Panner.)
Height, Joseph S. *Paradise on the Steppe: The Odyssey of a Pioneering People*. Bismark N.D.: North Dakota Historical Society of Germans From Russia, 1973.
Epp, G.K. "Mennonite-Ukrainian Relations 1789–1945." In *Journal of Mennonite Studies*, 7 (1989).

Baron von Haxthausen wrote of his impressions of the Mennonite lands in *Studies on the Interior of Russi.* Chicago: University of Chicago Press, 1972.

The references to the "Governing Senate in Petersburg" and to the proclamation regarding potatos are from *A Source Book for Russian History.* Edited by George Vernadsky. New Haven: Yale University Press, 1972.

For information about Mennonite and Ukrainian relations I read:

Brandes, Detlef. "German Colonists in Southern Ukraine up to the Repeal of the Colonial Statute." In *German-Ukrainian Relations in Historical Perspective.* Edited by John-Paul Himka and Hans-Joachim Torke. Toronto: CIUS Press, 1994. (This is also the source of Andreas Kappeler's "Ukrainians and Germans in Southern Ukraine 1870s to 1914" and the data of comparative literacy rates.)

The source of the anecdote about the song of the lark in the steppes and of the reference to the "Russians just need more threshings" is from the memoir:

Dyck, Arnold. *Lost in the Steppe.* Trans. Henry D. Dyck. Mansfield, Penn., 1974.

The poem by Taras Shevchenko, "Dedication," is from his collection *Kobzar* which has been published in countless editions in many languages. This version is my translation.

de Madaringa, Isabel. *Russia in the Age of Catherine the Great.* New Haven: Yale University Press, 1981. (This biographer of Catherine the Great cites Catherine's reference to "that political monstrosity, the 'Sech.'")

I also consulted:

Alexander, John T. *Catherine the Great: Life and Legend.* Oxford: Oxford University Press, 1989.

Erickson, Carolly. *Great Catherine.* New York: Crown, 1994.

Jejula, Heorhy. "Man Who Lived Through Three Centuries." *News From Ukraine* 3 (1988). (The source of the newspaper clipping that refers to the razing of the *sich.*)

Honchar, Oles. "The Cathedral." *Journal of Ukrainian Studies* (Fall 1976). (The source of the legend of the Cossack bell.)

The declaration of the historian Olena Apanovych appeared in *News From Ukraine* 3 (1990).

For the revolutionary period in Ukraine I read:

Footman, David. *Civil War in Russia.* New York: Praeger, 1962. (The source for the story of Makhno's estimation of Peter Kropotkin.)

Reshetar Jr., John. *The Ukrainian Revolution 1917–1920.* Princeton, N. J.: Princeton University Press, 1952. (The source of the observation that Makhno "mutilated" the Russian language and had a "burning desire to deliver orations.")

Pipes, Richard. *Russia Under the Bolshevik Regime*. New York: Knopf, 1993.
Volkogonov, Dimitri. *Trotsky: The Eternal Revolutionary*. New York: The Free Press, 1996. (This book cites Trotsky's telegram to Stalin.)

The basic texts for the *makhnoshchyna* are:
Arshinov. Peter. *The History of the Maknovist Movement*. Detroit: Black and Red, 1974. (First translated [into German] in 1923 by Voline.)
Voline. *The Unknown Revolution*. Montreal: Black Rose, 1975. (Equally foundational and the source of the speeches by Makhno, "On the contrary it strives to protect . . ." and "Let the noblemen and landlords beware.")
Other, scholarly, sources are:
Peters, Victor. *Nestor Makhno: The Life of an Anarchist*. Winnipeg: Echo Books, 1970.
Malet, Michael. *Nestor Makno in the Russian Civil War*. London: Macmillan, 1982.
Adams, Arthur E. "The Great Ukrainian Jacquerie." In *The Ukraine 1917–1920: A Study in Revolution*. Cambridge, Mass.: Harvard University Press, 1977.
The extracts from Makhno's memoirs were published as "Huliai-Pole" in *Ukraina* magazine (Kyiv: April 1991), with a commentary by the historian Valerii Volkovinskyi.

For Mennonite-Canadian literary versions of their history I read:
Reimer, Al. *My Harp Is Turned to Mourning*. Winnipeg: Hypernion, 1985. (This fictionalized account of the revolutionary period is the source of the reference to "angry crowds, ready for anything," "Someday he'd be a political leader," "fat pigs swimming in their own suet," ". . . a gory wake of death and destruction," "sneaky little *khokhol*" and "that cowardly pipsqueak?")
Weier, John. *Steppe: A Novel*. Winnipeg: Thistledown, 1995.
Wiebe, Rudy. *The Blue Mountains of China*. Toronto: NCL, 1995.
For the reminiscences of the schoolteacher Dietrich Neufeld:
Neufeld, Dietrich. *A Russian Dance of Death*. Trans. Al Reimer. Winnipeg: Hypernion, 1980.

About the *maknoshchyna* see:
Height, Joseph S. *Paradise on the Steppe*. (For "It was like a wolfhunt" and "To dance with the murderers.")

Smith, C. Henry. *The Story of the Mennonites*. (The source for the hyperbolic "almost unequalled among any civilized people" and for the references to the "pleasant interlude for Mennonites" and to the village of Orloff in 1938.)

# CREDITS

Permissions for quotes used in *The Doomed Bridegroom:*

Robin Morgan. *The Demon Lover: On the Sexuality of Terrorism.* Copyright © 1989 by Robin Morgan. Reprinted by permission of W. W. Norton & Company, Inc.

Mykhaylo Osadchy. *Cataract.* Translated by Marko Carynnyk. New York: Harcourt Brace Jovanovich, 1976. Reprinted by permission of the translator.

Kazimierz Orlos. "Barbed Wire Fox" from *Index on Censorship.* Reprinted by permission of Index on Censorship. This article originally appeared in Index on Censorship 3/84. For further information please contact: 33 Islington High Street, London, N1 9LH. Phone: 0171 278 2314, Fax: 0171 278 1878. Email: <contact@indexoncensorship.org>

John Weier. *Steppe: A Novel.* Thistledown Press, 1995. Reprinted with permission of Thistledown Press.

Rudy Wiebe. *The Blue Mountains of China.* Toronto: NCL 1995. Reprinted with permission of the author.

Elizabeth Wilson. "A New Romanticism?" from *The Left and the Erotic*, edited by Eileen Phillips. London: Lawrence & Wishart, 1983. Reprinted with permission of Lawrence & Wishart.

Vasyl Stus. *Vasyl Stus: Selected Poems.* Translated by Jaropolk Lassowsky. Munich: The Ukrainian Free University, 1987. Reprinted with permission of the Ukrainian Free University Press.

# PREVIOUS APPEARANCES

The Preface was published in *Mostovi*, a journal of literary translation. Trans. David Albahari. Belgrade (September 1997).

An earlier version of "The Collaborators" was adapted as a radio drama for the CBC program *Speaking Volumes* in 1989 and was also collected in *Out of Place.* Edited by `Ven Begamudre and Shelley Sopher. Regina: Coteau, 1991.

An earlier version of "Within the Copper Mountain" was published in *Why Are You Telling Me This? Eleven Acts of Intimate Journalism.* Edited by Barbara Moon et al. Banff: Banff Centre Press, 1997. It was also adapted for the CBC radio series *Ideas.* Produced by Kathleen Flaherty in 1997.